Peru

Peru

BY MARION MORRISON

*Enchantment of the World
Second Series*

Children's Press®

A Division of Grolier Publishing

NEW YORK   LONDON   HONG KONG   SYDNEY
DANBURY, CONNECTICUT

Frontispiece: A Peruvian girl with an alpaca

Consultant: Mary G. Berg, Lecturer in Latin American Studies, Harvard University

Please note: All statistics are as up-to-date as possible at the time of publication.

Visit Children's Press on the Internet: http://publishing.grolier.com

Book production by Herman Adler Design Group

Library of Congress Cataloging-in-Publication Data

Morrison, Marion.
    Peru / by Marion Morrison.
      p. cm. — (Enchantment of the world. Second series)
    Includes bibliographical references and index.
    Summary: Describes the geography, plants and animals, history,
economy, language, sports and arts, religions, culture, and people
of South America's third largest republic.
    ISBN 0-516-21545-0
    1. Peru—Juvenile literature. [1. Peru.] I. Series.
F3408.5.M67 2000
985—dc21
                              99-17871
                              CIP

Acknowledgments

The author wishes to thank the following people and organizations who were particularly helpful in the preparation of this volume. In Peru, Patricia Pianezzi de Rodgerson, Carmen Azurín, the late Eduardo Ronalds, Lolita Ronalds, *The Lima Times*, the National Library, Lima. In London, the cultural section of the Peruvian Embassy and the library of Canning House.

Contents

Cover photo:
Mooring a reed boat
in Lake Titicaca

Colca Valley

A golden mask

Mysteries
of Peru

On July 24, 1911, a young North American explorer was led to some ruins at the top of a hill overlooking the Urubamba Valley in southern Peru. Many of the ruins were covered in forest, but some had been cleared by local Native American families to grow crops. The explorer also saw walls made of large stone blocks, a religious sun stone, an area he called the "main court," stone houses with newly thatched roofs, stairways, and ruined buildings. The young explorer was Hiram Bingham and the site was Machu Picchu. That Inca city is now

Opposite: **A geoglyph on a hillside in Paracas**

The ancient Incan city of Machu Picchu in the Andes Mountains

so famous it is synonymous with Peru, and many people believe it is the most stunning archaeological site in the Americas.

Bingham's expedition had been looking for a "lost city" of the Inca—the refuge of the last members of the Inca empire as they fled from Spanish invaders. The Inca empire was centered on Cuzco, not far from Machu Picchu. In less than 300 years, it had expanded to include present-day Ecuador, southern Colombia, most of Bolivia, northern Argentina, and northern Chile.

Visitors to Peru can see many Inca sites, such as Cuzco with its great fortress of Sacsahuamán. Other sites include the nearby fountains and storehouses of Tambo Machay, the sun-stone of Kenko, the Temple of Viracocha at Raqchi, the agricultural terraces of Moray, and more.

Impressive as these historic sites are, Inca life is perhaps best reflected today in the life of the Quechua people, whose home is the Peruvian highlands. Descendants of the Inca and the people they conquered, their traditional way of life as farmers and herders has changed little over the centuries.

Fifteen years after Hiram Bingham first stood at Machu Picchu, another mystery began to unfold on the Peruvian coast. In September 1926 two archaeologists, one Peruvian and one North American, were searching around desert graves near the small town of Nazca. They scrambled up a hill to get a better view and noticed some strange markings on the desert surface. They made some notes but attached no great significance to the markings. In the 1940s, another archaeologist visited the site and took a different view. Believing the

Quechua people at the Chincheros village market in the Andean highlands

site represented a calendar, he declared it was "the largest astronomy book in the world."

Whatever the explanation, the "lines of Nazca" have become almost as famous as Machu Picchu. The Nazca were just one of several ancient coastal civilizations who have left a

Geopolitical map of Peru

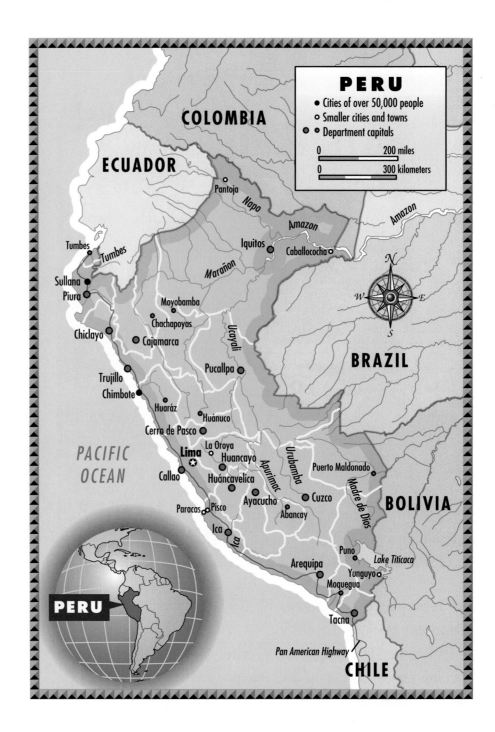

legacy to Peru of some of the most outstanding treasures in the Western world.

Today, the coast and the mountains continue to reveal secrets of the past. Frozen skeletons of Inca children have been discovered in snowy mountain summits. In the northern desert, the tomb of the Lord of Sipán, said to be the most fabulous treasure ever found in the Americas, was accidentally discovered by grave robbers in 1987. This royal tomb revealed a mass of gold artifacts, semiprecious gems, fine weavings, shells, and minerals. Other tombs full of treasures have been found since then.

For 200 years after the arrival of the Spaniards and the conquest of the Inca by Francisco Pizarro early in the sixteenth century, Peru was the most important region of the Spaniards' vast colonial empire. Its silver and gold mines were a source of enormous wealth to the Spanish Crown, and Lima was known as the "City of Kings." The Spaniards developed the land and established large estates, but the ordinary people suffered at their hands. Independence from Spain came in the early nineteenth century, and since then Peru has struggled to come to terms with its incredible past.

During the twentieth century, Peru was often governed by dictators or military men. It was also troubled by guerrilla movements, a failing economy, and the illegal cocaine trade. But since the 1990s, when Alberto Fujimori was elected president, the economy has improved and the guerrilla threat has lessened. In the twenty-first century, Peru's vast Amazon region, which has extensive deposits of oil and gas, may help provide a stable economy for this struggling nation.

Country
of Contrasts

P ERU IS SOUTH AMERICA'S THIRD-LARGEST COUNTRY. IT stretches southward from within 3 miles (5 kilometers) of the equator for 1,225 miles (1,971 km). Peru is famed for its desert, ranking among the driest places in the world. This long arid zone faces the Pacific Ocean on the west and flanks the Andes Mountains to the east. Lima, Peru's capital city, is in the center of the long desert.

Opposite: **Taray is a village in a valley near Mount Saguaciray.**

The mouth of the Ocono River

The Andean Mountain ranges, or *sierra*, form the backbone of the country. Peru's highest peak, Mount Huascarán, crowns the central chain at 22,205 feet (6,768 meters). The first recorded climb of the peak was made by North American Annie S. Peck in 1908.

To the east of the Andes lies the humid Amazonian forest. Much of the forested area is mountainous and is known as the *montaña*. The huge low-lying area around the Amazon is generally called the *selva*, meaning "jungle."

A path through the jungle near Puerto Maldonado

Peru is 854 miles (1,374 km) across at its widest point and has an area of 496,222 square miles (1,285,116 sq km)—almost twice the size of Texas. This incredible land contains what many scientists believe to be the world's greatest range of biodiversity.

The Long Desert

Apart from the mangrove-fringed estuary of the Tumbes River in the far north, the desert extends the full length of Peru's coast for approximately 1,500 miles (2,414 km). This great desert varies from 10 to 100 miles (16 to 160 km) wide, with the broadest sections in the far north and in the south.

The shifting sands of the Sechura Desert

The part known as the Sechura Desert lies virtually at sea level between the northern towns of Piura and Chiclayo. The Sechura is best known for its shifting sands, shallow borax lakes, scrub forests—and its isolation. Inca roads once skirted this desert, and the first Spanish invaders used them in their march southward to overwhelm the Native American kingdoms. Few people live in the Sechura today, but its deposits of phosphate rock are mined and used for fertilizer production.

Among other broad sections are the low tablelands near Ica, south of Lima. Farther south, parts of the desert widen and slope gently inland to higher altitudes, reaching 7,557 feet (2,303 m) near the city of Arequipa.

Peru's Geographical Features

Highest Elevation: Mount Huascarán, 22,205 feet (6,768 m) above sea level

Lowest Elevation: Sea level along the Pacific Coast

Longest Rivers: The Marañón and Ucayali Rivers, about 1,000 miles (1,609 km) long, meet near the foot of the Andes to form the Amazon.

Largest and Highest Lake: Lake Titicaca covers 3,200 square miles (8,287 sq km) on the border of Peru and Bolivia, with 1,914 square miles (4,957 sq km) in Peru. At 12,507 feet (3,812 m) above sea level, it is the world's highest navigable lake.

Greatest Annual Precipitation: More than 100 inches (254 cm) in Iquitos

Lowest Annual Precipitation: Less than 1 inch (2.5 cm) in Lima

Hottest Average Temperature: 95°F (35°C) in the tropical forests

Lowest Average Temperature: 47°F (8°C) in the mountains

Longest Shared Border: 1,803 miles (2,901 km), with Colombia

Coastline: 1,500 miles (2,414 km), along the Pacific Ocean

Greatest Distance North to South: 1,225 miles (1,971 km)

Greatest Distance East to West: 854 miles (1,374 km)

Deadliest Earthquake: About 70,000 people died in an earthquake in northern Peru on May 31, 1970.

The Humboldt Current

As the first explorers ventured southward in small sailing ships they found the sea unusually cool and often shrouded in mist.

Millions of seabirds gathered above rich schools of fish. There was almost no rain, and along the coast only river valleys carrying water from the mountains supported abundant life. In 1802, a Prussian traveler and scientist named Alexander von Humboldt checked the temperature of the sea. He found that it was about 8°F (-13°C) lower off the Peruvian coast than in similar latitudes elsewhere. He also found that the temperature of the air over the land was warmer than the sea.

Humboldt had discovered one of the conditions that created the desert, but it was many years before the total picture was understood. The cold ocean currents that bathe the Peruvian coast became known as the Humboldt Current, although today the name Peru Current is more often used. The cold water rises from an ocean trench close to the shore. The trench is often deeper than the mountains are high. Icy water wells upward from the trench to chill the surface and then sweeps northward toward the equator. Adding to the desert climate, the moist onshore winds blowing from the Pacific are cooled by the sea. A *thermal inversion* occurs, in which cooler air stays close to the surface and only the higher air is warmer. Fogs are common along the coast, but rain seldom occurs. The result is a lunar landscape of rocks and drifting sand.

Desert Valleys

Breaks in the long desert occur where rivers starting in the high Andes flow through valleys to the sea. These valleys have been cultivated for centuries. They were inhabited by ancient

El Niño

When a flow of warm water beginning near the equator in the Pacific Ocean replaces the cold Peru Current, several natural phenomena occur. The cool water is normally rich with plankton, but the plankton die when the water warms, leading to a sudden decline in the fish population. Without fish, millions of seabirds die. For many years this warm current has been known to Peruvians as *El Niño*, a shortened form of *El Niño Jesús* (The Baby Jesus), because the warming usually happens around Christmas. The term *El Niño* is now widely used to describe the climatic conditions that have brought destruction and flooding in many parts of the world.

Colca Valley

civilizations like the Nazca and the Moche. Some valleys, such as the Chicama in the north and the Ica in the south, are broad. Others are little more than rocky gorges where life clings to damp soil. Not all the rivers flow with water every year because the rain in the mountains is not always heavy in the same place. On the other hand, the valleys sometimes flood after torrential rain in the heights.

In a few parts of the coast, the fog is so dense at times that enough water condenses to allow plants to grow. In these very moist areas, known to the Peruvians as *lomas*, there may even be trees and enough grass for cattle to graze on. Like the rest of the coast, the lomas are affected by changes in the Peru Current.

Looking at Peru's Cities

At an altitude of 7,557 feet (2,303 m) above sea level, Arequipa sits at the foot of El Misti, a volcano in southeastern Peru. Average temperatures there range from about 54°F (12°C) in July to about 60°F (16°C) in January. Founded in 1540 by Francisco Pizarro, Arequipa is now the chief trading center for southern Peru. Textile mills, soap production, and tourism are the main industries. Many of Arequipa's buildings were built from light-colored volcanic rock called sillar, and the city is nicknamed the "White City" because many of them shine in the sun.

Callao lies on Callao Bay just west of Lima. Founded in 1537, Callao is now Peru's chief seaport. Near the port, shipyards build fishing vessels. Metalworking, breweries, and fish-meal production are other important industries. The Real Felipe Fort military post, which is open to visitors, houses the Museum of Military History in its old barracks.

Chiclayo is in northwestern Peru near the Pacific Ocean. Founded in the 1560s by Spanish priests, Chiclayo is one of Peru's fastest-growing cities today and is the commercial center of northwestern Peru. Mercado Modelo is a lively outdoor market with stalls filled with handicrafts and a section called the *mercado de brujos* (witch doctors' market). Chiclayo's foods and music combine the area's African and Indian heritages.

The Andes

It is difficult to visit Peru without noticing the Andes Mountains. Lima stands at the very foot of the *sierra* on a bed of alluvial rock formed by the Rimac River, and frequent earth tremors remind residents that the Andes are still growing. The mountains are young in geological terms—only 40 million to 60 million years old.

At one time the South American continent tilted toward the west—the Pacific—but that has changed. As the Andes rose,

A street in an Andean village today

the continent tilted the other way. The Amazon waters now drain east, while the remains of ancient beaches lie far above the shoreline on the west. Relics of sea life, such as fish, mammals, and mollusks, are found far inland.

The modern Peruvian Andes are just part of a chain that stretches 4,500 miles (7,242 km) along the western side of South America. In Peru itself, the range can be divided into three parts. The northern section is narrow and low from east to west. The central section is a mass of high mountain ranges with many snowcapped peaks. It includes the highest, broad fertile valleys and the main source of the Amazon River. Some parts of this section are very remote, and the land is so rugged and uneven that a bus journey of 100 miles (160 km) can take all day. West of the central ranges, Mount Huascarán dominates the permanently snow-covered Cordillera Blanca.

A Quechua woman herding livestock below Nevado Ausangate, near the Cordillera Carabaya

1970 Earthquake

An earthquake in 1970 dislodged part of Mount Huascarán's glacier, causing an avalanche of mud, ice, and rock to sweep down into the valley below. More than half the city of Huaráz was destroyed (right) and half the population died, but worst hit was the town of Yungay, which completely disappeared. Only the tops of four palm trees that stood in the main square could be seen once the mud had settled, and this part of the town has now been turned into a cemetery. Some 70,000 people are thought to have lost their lives in the earthquake. Nearby stands the old cemetery, a few feet higher than the rest of the town. A handful of residents stranded there miraculously survived the disaster.

The Andean ranges are broadest in the southern section, reaching up to 400 miles (644 km) from east to west. Most of the ranges on the west are volcanic, with some perfect cones such as that of El Misti, which overlooks Arequipa, and Peru's most active volcano, Ubinas. These volcanoes are so close to the desert conditions of the west that in some years they are totally devoid of snow.

Most of the eastern ranges are older, much more rugged, and snowcapped. The greatest of all is the most easterly of the Peruvian mountains—the Cordillera Carabaya, with peaks reaching more than 19,000 feet (5,791 m).

Sabancaya Volcano, near Arequipa

Lake Titicaca

Andean Lakes

Between the southern ranges lies a relatively unbroken high land called the *altiplano*. Much of this region slopes southward and drains into Lake Titicaca, the world's highest navigable lake. It is South America's largest lake after Lake Maracaibo in Venezuela. Lake Titicaca lies partly in Bolivia.

There are also innumerable small lakes in the Peruvian Andes. Some, like those near Huascarán, lie in glacial valleys. They are filled with a milky blue water from active glaciers. Others are merely shallow lagoons in the valleys between mountain ranges.

The Montaña

More than three-fifths of Peru lies east of the Andes. The mountains, which are so dry on the western side, are richly forested on the east. There is no hard-and-fast rule, but generally the cool, dryer mountain vegetation of grasses and small plants extends downward to about 8,200 feet (2,500 m). There, the scenery begins to change. The line is usually very clear as grasses give way to low bushes and shrubs. This is known as the *ceja de la montaña*—literally, the "eyebrow, or fringe, of the forest." The line marks the point where moisture and warmth rising from the Amazonian forest below allow a richer growth. Often the mountain slopes are steep, and the vegetation can be seen thickening with every few feet of changing altitude.

The annual rainfall in the eastern, forested mountain area known as the *montaña* is measured in feet, and mudslides are frequent. Thousands of trees, along with millions of tons of soil, may slip without warning, obliterating trails and homes.

A high Andes waterfall in Manu National Park

The steep mountainsides lead to relatively flat land at an altitude of approximately 500 feet (152 m). The land then slopes gently eastward to an altitude of 260 feet (79 m) at the Peru-Brazil border. Close to the foot of the mountains, the major rivers may be almost 1 mile (1.6 km) wide. From there, they follow a shallow, meandering course through the forests. This part of the *montaña*, particularly the great flatlands of Loreto and Madre de Dios, is known as the *selva*.

An Amazon tributary follows a meandering course through a rain forest.

Boats are sometimes the only means of transportation in the Iquitos suburb of Belem.

Amazon Tributaries

The lush eastern slopes of the Andes are broken by numerous valleys, swift rivers with rapids, canyons, and high waterfalls. All the rivers flow to the great Amazon system, and most head northeast to the main Amazon River in Brazil.

The Apurimac River, the Amazon's longest tributary, begins in the Peruvian Andes. The source, which is no more than a series of rivulets, is less than 90 miles (145 km) from the Pacific in the ranges of Chila near the village of Cailloma, within sight of the volcanoes. It is close to the source of the Colca River, which drains to the west through one of the world's deepest canyons.

The Selva

The forested lowlands of the selva are the least-developed region of Peru. There are just two major towns or cities—Iquitos and Pucallpa. Iquitos, the largest city in Peru's Amazon, is 1,268 miles (2,041 km) overland from Lima. Iquitos can be reached only by air or by river, however, because there are no roads through the surrounding dense forests. The nearest large town is Pucallpa, on the Ucayali River southwest of Iquitos. Pucallpa is connected to Lima by a trans-Andean road and by riverboat traffic to Iquitos—

Chachapoyas—The Cloud Forest People

An area of northern Peru is named *Chachapoyas* after an ancient people who lived there. These people are sometimes referred to as the "cloud forest people" because they lived in the mist-covered *ceja de la montaña*. Relatively little is known about them because their homelands are so remote and isolated. They were never completely conquered by the Inca, or discovered by the Spaniards. What remains of their civilization now lies in ruins—most yet to be uncovered—of towns and cities, houses, ceremonial centers, and fortresses.

a three- to seven-day journey depending on the height of the river. In the dry season, numerous sandbanks and the stranded, leafless remains of huge trees make navigation hazardous.

The sand is new sediment washed down from the Andes every year in swirling floodwaters. At Iquitos, the level of the Amazon can rise by as much as 40 feet (12 m) during February and March. Older sediments lie below the forest, the deeper levels being more ancient than the Andes Mountains. Geologists have found natural gas and oil in these deep sedimentary beds, but the distance from any major industrial center and the lack of good roads have delayed the development of these resources.

Land of Three Worlds

J UST AS PERU'S GEOGRAPHY VARIES FROM THE COASTAL desert to the Andean sierras to the lush Amazon selva, so too does wildlife vary around the country. Each region has its own specialized plants and animals that have adapted to local conditions.

Opposite: **Frogs among wild berries along the Madre de Dios River**

The Coast

For mile after mile, the desert coast of Peru is a dry wilderness. Although there is occasional rain, such as in years of El Niño, the land is virtually barren. The plants of this area are well adapted to the arid landscape. Some, such as cacti, are seen all year. They flower in the southern summer between January and March. Among the best-known cactus plants are the opuntias,

An opuntia cactus

which have flat-padded, spiny shapes. These plants grow mostly along the edges of valleys, where they are used as fences. The opuntia is known for its medicinal purposes, its edible fruits, and—in some places—for the tiny cochineal insects found living on the pads. The insects are used to make a rich red dye.

Another cactus well known to rural Peruvians is the San Pedro cactus. Its slender, cylindrical form is about 8 feet (2.4 m) high and has been used in Native American magic for at least 2,000 years. Many other cacti are smaller and far less obvious. Some lie close to the ground in long straggling shapes. A few are no bigger than a button and some have small flattened pads that minimize water loss.

In the coastal valleys, however, there is enough water to give a great variety of plants a chance to grow. Low trees with deep roots can find a foothold in the driest riverbeds. Most are specialized pod-bearing trees such as the algarrobo, known for its very hard wood and the Native American medicine made from its seeds. Numerous small mimosas with tiny leaves are found in this region, including the sensitive mimosa, whose leaves fold tightly when touched.

Peruvians in the desert valleys use small bromeliads to create patterns, especially slogans and advertisements. These plants, which are related to Spanish moss, have tough leaves with tiny scales. The bromeliad has almost no roots and gets its moisture from the foggy air.

Sloths—mammals of tropical South and Central America—are found in a few places in the warmer northern

valleys, along with monkeys and deer. Foxes and small rodents live in the desert, but the largest mammals are restricted to the seashore. Tens of thousands of seals and sea lions live along the coast. Some rocky places are so crowded that there is hardly a square inch of empty space.

Seals lounge on a rock in Paracas National Park as seabirds perch above them.

A Visit to the Bird Islands

Peru has a number of small islands lying close to the shore. For centuries these have been nesting grounds for millions of seabirds. Gannets, cormorants, and pelicans live on fish that, in turn, are dependent on the plankton. The dry coastal climate preserved deep beds of guano (bird excrement), which the Inca used to fertilize their crops. In the nineteenth century, guano export became a major industry, and today the stocks are depleted. The combined impact of industrial fishing and El Niño have drastically reduced Peru's bird population.

Many of the guano islands are now closed to visitors in an effort to prevent disturbance of the remaining colonies, but a trip to the Ballestas Islands near Pisco, about 150 miles (240 km) south of Lima, is a popular tourist attraction. The sea is smooth and the waters are clear and cool. Birds dive into the sea for fish with pinpoint accuracy. Long skeins of cormorants and pelicans skim over the surface. The excursion boats pass close to seals, sea lions, and Humboldt penguins (above) scrambling along rocks near the water's edge.

Life in the Lomas

As many as sixty species of plants have been found in the foggy *lomas* on the desert coast. Trees grow in some lomas, and moisture condensing on their leaves drips to the ground, giving life to a green carpet of mosses and ferns below. The lomas are home to many species of birds often found in the valleys but not normally seen in the desert. One of the most colorful is the tiny vermilion flycatcher. Small doves, plovers, and migrants such as cuckoos are other birds of the lomas.

The Sierra

East of the desert, the Andes Mountains rise like a wall. In a few places north of Lima it is possible to see snowcaps and desert sand at the same time. In northern Peru, where the mountains are lower and the climate is wetter, the hillsides are green. The vegetation there consists of small plants that grow close to the ground with a variety of larger species in the valleys. Locally these greener places are known as *jalcas*.

The climate in the central sierra tends to be drier, and droughts are often severe in the south. Most of the central and southern mountains are treeless except on the montaña slope. Slow-growing trees, largely of the rose family, stood here at one time, but most have been cut down since Europeans arrived. Relics of the forests exist in a few isolated places, and some are now being protected. The most noticeable trees today are the tall eucalypti, which were introduced from Australia more than a century ago. Few other plants are tall, the exception being the giant *Puya raimondii*.

The Puya—Pineapple's Giant Cousin

Except for one African species, bromeliads are plants of the Americas. They exist in many forms, from the straggly Spanish moss to the pineapple with its succulent fruit to the *Puya raimondii*, which has a tall central flower stalk. This huge bromeliad, named after nineteenth-century Italian traveler Antonio Raimondi, easily reaches a height of more than 30 feet (9.1 m) and is claimed to be the world's tallest spike of flowers. It grows only in a few parts of the Andes, and one of the best places to see it is in on the rugged slopes of the Cordillera Blanca, where scattered groups stand out against the yellow mountain grasses.

The leafy lower part of the plant is taller than the average human. The leaves are tough, with sharp spines along the edges. These spines snare unwary predators such as small hawks hunting the smaller birds that nest in the Puya.

The plant takes many years to develop, and then the flower spike shoots upward in a matter of months. More than 8,000 tiny flowers cover the central column and bear millions of feathery light seeds. The Puya flowers just once and then dies. Occasionally, local Native Americans light the dry, dead plant like a gigantic candle at fiesta times.

Grasslands locally known as *punas* cover the higher mountain slopes. Bogs and small lakes with specialized plants fill the high valleys. Rivers cut their way down the mountains in valleys or canyons. Some are so deep that the vegetation at the top of the canyon is adapted to mountain cold while at the bottom the vegetation is subtropical, adapted to the mild air.

Few people live above 14,000 feet (4,267 m), partly because the highlands are so bleak, and also because there is less oxygen at higher altitudes. Animal life here is sparse and specialized. Several small rodents, including guinea pigs, are natives of the Andes. Birds are mostly small too. Because there are no trees, one species of woodpecker—the Andean flicker—nests in earthen banks, such as the sides of dry riverbeds. The master of these skies is the giant Andean condor, a vulture with a wingspan of 10 feet (3 m). Condors nest on rocky mountain ledges and use thermal air currents to soar around the mountaintops or fly to the coast, where they feed on dead seals or other carrion. In the mountains, their best chance of a meal is the carcass of one of the rare Andean deer or one of the Andean animals related to camels.

Llamas are members
of the camel family.

Llamas, called "Peruvian sheep" by the first Europeans, are members of the camel family. They were domesticated long ago, and their wool and meat have been used for centuries. The wool is spun by hand, dyed, and woven into fine cloth. Llamas are also used for carrying light loads. They have a place in local folklore, and at one time many were sacrificed at festivals. Even today the form of a llama is said to appear in constellations of stars much as, in the Northern Hemisphere, people see the signs of the zodiac.

The alpaca, a slightly smaller cousin of the llama, is also domesticated and is kept largely for its wool. The llama also has two

A thirteen-year-old boy takes
care of several alpacas.

The Vicuña

The vicuña is the smallest of the Andean camel relatives. A fully grown male vicuña is little more than 3 feet (91 centimeters) high at the shoulder. They have a long neck, golden brown fleece, and pointed ears. Vicuñas live in small groups of up to fifteen females with one male and are found only in the highest grasslands. They are fast runners, but because of the value of their wool they have been poached almost to extinction in many parts of the sierra.

Vicuña wool has been used for weaving since Inca times, but in those days, the animals were well protected. They were rounded up and sheared each year, but afterward, they were returned to the wild. Only chosen women were allowed to work with the wool, making wonderfully soft garments for the Inca nobles. In the twentieth century, hunters and poachers reduced the numbers of vicuña until the animals were almost wiped out. In the 1960s, backed by Peru's government and international agencies, Peruvian zoologists created reserves where the vicuña could be protected, notably at Pampas Galeras in the mountains above Nazca. New laws made it a criminal offense to kill a vicuña. The measures were successful, and vicuña are now surviving in good numbers.

wild relatives—the vicuña and the guanaco. Guanacos are quite rare in Peru, however, and are seldom seen except in remote parts of the southern highlands.

The Eastern Slopes

From the eyebrow of the forest on the eastern side of the Andes Mountains, down the slope, and out to the flat Amazon River Basin, wildlife becomes progressively more exuberant. The number of species increases, and it takes only a moment to realize there is a constant buzz of insects in this powerhouse of life. The great diversity of wildlife is partly due to the range of altitudes and also because Peru's position in the Andes makes it a meeting place for species coming from both north and south. This incredible variety of species makes Manu National Park one of the world's most valuable wildlife reserves.

Amazon Lowlands

The enormous expanse of selva in the Amazon lowlands is a wonderland of plants. Some areas have the characteristically tall, buttressed trees of the rain forest. Some of these, such as the Lupunas, grow 150 feet (46 m) high. Their tall straight trunks have no branches except at the top, where the crown emerges from a surrounding canopy of leafy, lower trees. From the higher branches, long trailing vines called lianas stretch to the ground. They grow from seeds deposited by birds.

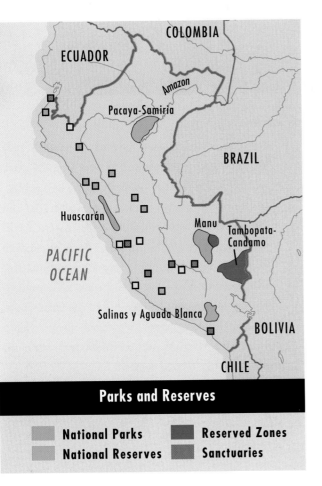

Parks and Reserves

National Parks
National Reserves
Reserved Zones
Sanctuaries

A Wildlife El Dorado

Manu National Park, known simply as Manu, covers 7,263 square miles (18,811 sq km) of eastern Peru. It is a little smaller than New Jersey. The name comes from a sluggish Amazon tributary running southeast along the foot of the Andes. Manu begins high in the mountains just above the eyebrow zone and includes the steep slope and numerous mountain streams that feed the river. Rainfall in the highlands is low, but in the forest it can be as much as 156 inches (396 cm) annually.

Vegetation ranges from puna grasses, to the low rosette plants of the jalcas, to the eyebrow of stunted trees and bushes, to moss, to fern-draped cloud forest with 20-foot (6-m)-high giant tree ferns, to giant buttressed trees of the tropical rain forest. Much of the park is still unexplored, but scientists estimate that more than 1,000 species of birds live there. For bird-watchers, the most unforgettable sight may be hundreds of macaws gathered on a mud bank rich with salt.

Thirteen species of primates, including tiny marmosets and larger black spider monkeys, have been reported. Giant otters up to 7 feet (2 m) long hunt for fish and play in lagoons. Caimans—South American crocodilians—and river turtles live beside the river, while jaguars, ocelots, sloths, armadillos, and anteaters inhabit the forest.

Parts of Manu are open to the public, but most of it is off-limits to all but scientists. The park is recognized by the United Nations Educational, Scientific, and Cultural Organization (UNESCO) as the Manu Biosphere Reserve.

Toucans live in the rain forest canopy.

The canopy is rich with life. Trees flower here, and plants such as bromeliads and mosses grow in profusion. Many birds inhabit the canopy. Among the largest are parrots, macaws, toucans, eagles, and vultures. The smaller species include many hummingbirds, some of the tiniest of all birds. The ground below the trees is dank, and fallen vegetation rots quickly due to the wealth of bacteria, fungi, and insects. Smaller rodents such as agoutis and pacas find a ready larder

of grubs and tender shoots on the ground. These dark areas of the forest are also home to wild pigs, snakes, and lizards. Most of the species found in Manu may also be seen here, but human activity has taken a toll. Large caimans are no longer common, and neither are certain monkeys and rodents that are good to eat.

The collared peccary is a wild pig that has four toes on its forelegs and only three on its hind legs.

All of the selva is not covered with tall forest, though. Some areas have mile after mile of palm forest and small, open lagoons. The water is often stained dark from rotting vegetation, and leaves of aquatic plants lie on the surface.

The Park of Legends

Lima began to expand in the late 1950s as it drew people from around the country. They came from the mountains, the coast, and the selva. The Park of Legends was born from the idea that people from each area should have a chance to understand something about the homeland of their neighbors. The park was originally set at the edge of Lima, but the city has grown to surround it. It is home to many animals and plants from many places. Macaws sit in trees almost at touching distance, monkeys have their own island, and there are some museum exhibits. A genuine pre-Hispanic adobe pyramid forms part of the site. On weekends the park is packed, and a craft market is busy. The goods, like the people, come from throughout Peru.

The Golden Kingdoms

P EOPLE LIVED ON THE COAST AND IN THE MOUNTAINS OF Peru long before the Inca. The first inhabitants of North and South America came from Asia sometime during the last Ice Age. They are believed to have crossed a land bridge over the Bering Strait. They survived as nomadic hunters, gatherers, and fishers. From about 2000 B.C., people living in the valleys of the desert coast grew cotton, maize, squash, peppers, beans, and nuts. They made simple weavings and pots. In the mountains, people used primitive forms of irrigation to cultivate potatoes and cereals. They used llamas to carry these crops, which they traded with people on the coast.

By about 900 to 800 B.C., the Indian cultures began to produce fine pottery and build large ceremonial structures. They were also expert weavers. The first of these cultures developed around the ceremonial center of Chavín de Huantar in the mountains and at Cerro Sechín on the coast. The Chavin were known for their artistic ceramics and the widespread use of feline motifs, while at Sechín, stone walls with carvings of macabre heads and warriors remain from one of the largest early buildings in Peru.

Opposite: **A gold mask of the Mochica people**

A carving of a head from the Chavin culture

A mummy of an adult male of the Paracas culture

In the 1920s, a burial ground was discovered at Paracas, on the southern coast, with more than 400 mummies dating back to about 600 B.C. They were wrapped in some of the finest weavings ever produced in the ancient world and were preserved in excellent condition because of the dryness of the desert. South of Paracas lies the Nazca Valley, where a civilization distinguished for its weaving and pottery lasted to about A.D. 500.

The Moche ruled much of the north coast of Peru from about A.D. 100 to 700. They were skilled engineers who used canals and aqueducts for irrigation and created an excellent road network. Their two main pyramids—the Pyramid of the Sun and the Pyramid of the Moon—were huge.

The Mystery of the Nazcas

The ancient Nazca civilization is best known for the lines and drawings of animals—including a spider, a monkey, a whale, and birds—that cover a large area of the desert around their valley. The Nazca created the lines by removing dark stones to expose the lighter sandy ground underneath. The intriguing lines and drawings are best seen from a hill or from the air. Since they were first recorded in the 1920s, many people have tried to explain their significance. One German mathematician spent more than fifty years in the desert making calculations relating the lines to stars and constellations. Other experts have used computers and

researched Indian spiritual thinking to find an explanation. Many of the lines can be linked to important Indian shrines such as the source of a spring of water, or the top of a hill.

The Moche Pyramid
of the Moon

More than 140 million adobe bricks were used to build the Pyramid of the Sun. The Moche were also excellent potters and goldsmiths who made exquisite ornaments in gold, silver, and precious stones. They created pots that looked like human faces and decorated others with everyday scenes, including medical operations and themes of war and warriors.

The Moche Empire ended with a famine caused by El Niño. Much of Peru then came under the influence of the highland Huari and Tiahuanaco cultures. Huari had its center near the modern city of Ayacucho. The ruins of Tiahuanaco, the highest urban center in the New World, still stand near the southern end of Lake Titicaca in Bolivia.

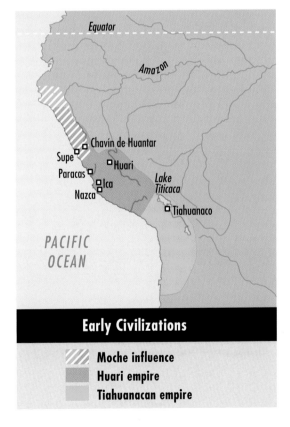

Early Civilizations

///// **Moche influence**
▓ **Huari empire**
░ **Tiahuanacan empire**

When the Huari culture ended around 1000, the Chimu, the strongest of the coastal cultures, developed along the north coast into the largest kingdom in Peru. The Chimu capital was the mud-brick city of Chan Chan, which dates from around 850 or 900. Successive rulers built new quarters for themselves and their nobles in Chan Chan, so that the walled city became a massive labyrinth of houses, rooms, and passageways that can still be defined on the site today. Artisans lived around the compound, weaving and crafting pots and metal objects needed by the court. The Chimu created their empire with strong, well-disciplined armies. But they were no match for the Inca, who conquered them in the middle of the fifteenth century.

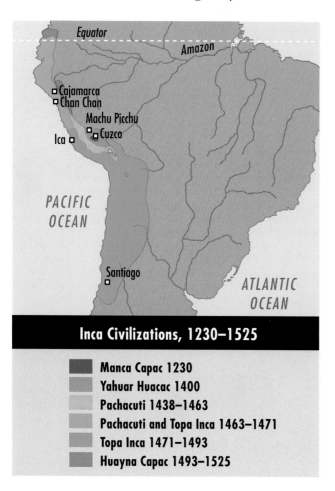

Inca Civilizations, 1230–1525

▮	Manca Capac 1230
▮	Yahuar Huacac 1400
▮	Pachacuti 1438–1463
▮	Pachacuti and Topa Inca 1463–1471
▮	Topa Inca 1471–1493
▮	Huayna Capac 1493–1525

The Inca

The Inca created the largest empire in the Americas in less than 300 years. In the 1200s, they were one of a number of small tribes in the Cuzco region. Gradually they subdued their neighbors. In 1438, the great Inca Pachacuti came to the throne. Most of the expansion of the empire was due to Pachacuti, his son Topa Inca, and his grandson Huayna Capac.

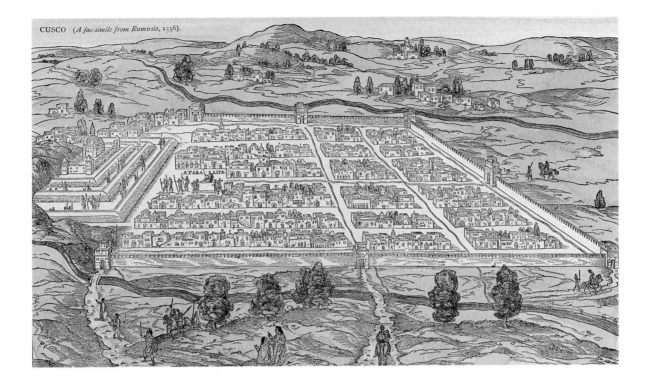

CUSCO (*A fac-simile from Ramusio,* 1556).

The Inca Empire was centered on Cuzco and divided into four parts roughly equivalent to the points of the compass. Well-maintained roads reached every part of the empire. Every few kilometers there were storehouses stocked with food and textiles that could be used by the Inca on their travels or by their army, which then could move quickly over long distances. The storehouses also fed the *chasquis,* or teams of runners who carried messages across the empire. Running as fast as they could, the chasquis traveled approximately four times faster than a horseman and are said to have carried fresh fish from the coast to Cuzco for dinner.

Local communities shared their food at festivals held in honor of their gods. Generally the sick and elderly were cared for by the state. In return, the people worked hard.

The city of Cuzco during Inca rule

Quinoa (left) and maize (right) were important Inca crops.

Most of the population contributed to the production of food. Growing crops on the steep slopes of the Andes without knowledge of the wheel could not have been easy. But the Inca overcame these problems by using irrigation, cutting terraces into the slopes, and adopting the llama as a beast of burden. The main crops were maize, which originally was introduced from Mexico, potatoes, beans, and native cereals such as quinoa.

Farming was one way many people contributed to the *mita*, a form of tax through labor that everyone was obliged to do for the good of the state. Others worked in the mines or as weavers. Materials such as llama wool and cotton were supplied by the state. Clothing was simple, though woven cloth could be brightly colored and patterned. Both sexes wore sleeveless tunics, with a cloak or mantle over the shoulders. A man's tunic

An eighteenth-century engraving of Inca worshiping the sun in characteristic tunics

was knee-length and worn over a loincloth, while a woman's was ankle-length with a wide belt or sash at the waist.

The Inca were expert stonemasons. The massive blocks they used were probably shaped by implements made of even harder rock. They had no metal tools or weapons. What is particularly remarkable about their buildings is that the blocks are so closely fitted together without mortar that it is not possible to pass a knife blade between them.

When the Inca won new territories they moved groups of people around to ensure loyalty. A trusted group from an already conquered area would be placed among new, less loyal tribes, while discontented enemies would be located where someone

An Inca *quipu* was used by trained experts to keep records.

Ice Maidens

Frozen mummies have been discovered near the summits of mountains in Peru and Chile, supporting the view that the Inca sacrificed victims to their gods—in this case to mountain gods. The most recent find was on 18,600-foot (5,669-m) Mount Pichu Pichu in southern Peru, where graves revealed the body of a fifteen-year-old girl. Her head had been deformed into a conical shape, she was wrapped in delicate cloth, and she had rubber sandals on her feet. With other mummies, archaeologists also found small statues: a gold female figure, a silver man, a gold vicuña, and a llama made of oyster shell, all gifts to the gods.

could keep an eye on them. As a common language, the Inca adopted Quechua from the local tribes. Curiously, the Inca had no known form of writing, though stories and legends were sung or passed down through the generations, and patterns on woven cloth often told a story. To keep accounts and records the Inca used a *quipu*, a device made of colored, knotted strings. Special experts, or quipu-keepers, were trained to use and understand them.

By 1532, the Inca empire extended from central Chile to southern Colombia. The difficulty of controlling such a large area led to the creation of a second capital in Quito, in what is now Ecuador. Inca ruler Huayna Capac moved to Quito because he was having trouble with the northern tribes, but he became ill, probably from smallpox, and died. Conflict arose over who should be his successor. Should it be his legitimate son, Huascar, who had been left in Cuzco to look after that part of the empire, or Huascar's half-brother Atahualpa, who was with Huayna Capac in Quito? Civil war broke out, and the empire was in chaos when the Spaniards arrived.

The Spanish Conquest

Francisco Pizarro, a farmer turned soldier and explorer, first found evidence of the great Inca empire when he landed in Tumbes in 1525. He then returned to Spain to organize an expedition to explore further. It was his great fortune to arrive back in Peru in 1532 when the Inca empire was divided. Huascar was dead but Atahualpa, now emperor, still feared his supporters. Hearing of the arrival of the Spaniards, and believing them to be white, bearded men of legendary fame, Atahualpa agreed to a meeting.

Francisco Pizarro

The Spaniards knew that their small number of men—less than 180—would fare badly against Atahualpa's thousands of troops, so they planned an ambush. When the Inca emperor entered the town of Cajamarca in northern Peru, there was no one to greet him. Eventually a Spanish priest approached, a bible in his hand. He showed the bible to Atahualpa, who looked through it with interest, not having seen a book before. He then threw it on the ground. This brought the offended Spaniards from their hiding places. They captured Atahualpa and took him prisoner. The Spaniards demanded a huge amount of gold for his release, but failed to keep their word when it was delivered, and Atahualpa was killed.

Pizarro knew he could claim the Inca Empire only if he took Cuzco, the capital and most sacred Inca city. Cuzco was many days' march from Cajamarca. On the way, he met some resistance from Atahualpa's supporters, but other tribes welcomed the emperor's death. The Spaniards also had the advantage of steel weapons and horses. Pizarro entered Cuzco in August 1533. The Spaniards were amazed at the city's wealth and helped themselves to its treasures. Pizarro agreed that Manco, one of Huayna Capac's sons, should become the new Inca leader, although with no real power. Pizarro returned to the coast to found Lima as the new capital in 1535.

Manco soon became aware of the Spaniards' real intentions. Not only did they mean to remain in his kingdom, but the conquistadors were rewarded by Pizarro with grants of land. To work the land, they enslaved the Native American peoples in a notorious system known as the *encomienda*. In theory the Spaniards were supposed to offer Christian teaching in exchange for the labor. Manco gathered his troops together and rebelled. A lengthy battle over the great fortress of Sacsahuamán, overlooking Cuzco, eventually was won by the Spaniards. Manco fled into the jungle and established a "court-in-exile" at Vitcos in the Vilcabamba Valley.

Ruins of the fortress of Sacsahuamán in Cuzco

Diego de Almagro, Pizarro's original partner in the Peru expedition, helped to lead the Spaniards to victory in Cuzco. Later the two men could not agree on how to divide the empire between them, and Pizarro and his brothers arranged Almagro's murder. Three years later, in 1541, Pizarro was murdered by supporters of Almagro.

Manco continued to hassle the Spaniards from his jungle exile but eventually was treacherously killed by some Spaniards he had befriended. He was succeeded by his son and, later, by his grandson. In 1572, during the governorship

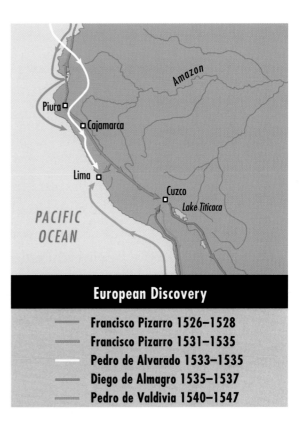

European Discovery

— Francisco Pizarro 1526–1528
— Francisco Pizarro 1531–1535
— Pedro de Alvarado 1533–1535
— Diego de Almagro 1535–1537
— Pedro de Valdivia 1540–1547

Cuzco, Qosqo—the Inca Capital

Cuzco is now often called by its old Quechua name—Qosqo. In its center is the main square, which in Inca times was surrounded by palaces, where many ceremonies and executions—including that of Tupac Amaru—took place. Today, instead of palaces, a cathedral and the Jesuit Church of La Compañia (right) stand on the square. The church is said to be the most beautiful in the city, with finely carved balconies and altars covered in gold leaf. Narrow cobblestone streets lined with Inca and Spanish buildings lead from the square. The Spaniards gave up trying to destroy all Cuzco's large stone buildings and instead built their own churches and palaces on top of the Inca walls. The Spanish Church of Santo Domingo, for instance, is built

above the Inca Sun Temple, the most revered shrine of the Inca Empire. Remarkably, in the great earthquake of 1650 and many others, the Inca walls have remained standing, while colonial and modern buildings have collapsed.

of Francisco de Toledo, the Inca were finally crushed and Manco's grandson Tupac Amaru, the last of the Inca, was put to death.

The Spanish Colony

The foundations of the Spanish colony were laid by Francisco de Toledo, who was viceroy of Peru from 1569 to 1581. Colonial Peru included present-day Bolivia. This mountainous area was of supreme importance because of a rich silver mine discovered in Potosi in 1545.

In 1545, a rich silver mine was discovered in Potosi, which is now part of Bolivia.

The colony was geared to fulfill the needs and greed of the Spanish conquerors and the Spanish king. Toledo extended the *encomienda* and built on the *mita* tax system of the Inca. Local chiefs were nominated as officials to collect taxes, and many did so ruthlessly. Every year, families—men, women, and children—were forced to leave their villages to make the trek hundreds of miles to Potosi.

At an altitude of more than 13,700 feet (4,176 m), Potosi is one of the highest cities in the world. To reach it more than 450 years ago was a horrendous journey on foot across mountains in freezing cold temperatures. Even if they completed the journey, the brutal and continuous work underground in the mine led to thousands of deaths. Eventually, as it became more difficult to get local labor, African slaves were brought in.

Other Native Americans were forced to pay their tax by working in textile workshops or were sent to the hot lowlands to cultivate plantations of coca. Coca leaves are part of the traditional life of Andean natives, helping to stave off hunger and tiredness, and the Spaniards made good profits from the industry. Toledo also introduced *reducciones*—centers like small towns based on the Spanish system of a central square, a church, a town council, and a prison. This meant moving communities of people around again, but made it easier for the Spaniards to collect taxes.

The population began to change as the number of Native American peoples declined in the sixteenth and seventeenth centuries. While many thousands died of overwork, even more succumbed to diseases brought by the Europeans, such as smallpox and flu. Others, by association with Spanish settlers, gave birth to a new, mixed group of people called *mestizos*. The Spaniards themselves fell into two groups: *peninsulares*, who were Spaniards born in Spain but living in the colonies, and *criollos*, Spaniards born in the colonies. This white minority dominated life in the colony.

By the 1700s, colonial society was well established. The Viceroyalty of Peru covered most of the Spanish-speaking territories in South America, with Lima as its capital. Lima flourished from taxes on trade, all of which passed through the city en route to Spain. This included merchandise from as far away as Buenos Aires, on the other side of South America.

Toward the end of the century, the Native Americans tired of the restrictions, the taxes, and the exploitation, and in Peru they rebelled against the Spanish. They were led by a mestizo named Tupac Amaru II, who claimed to be descended from Tupac Amaru, the last Inca. The revolt was put down, and Tupac Amaru, like his namesake, was executed in Cuzco's main plaza. But the Spanish monarchy took note and did allow an easing of trade restrictions and curtailed some of the worst Spanish excesses.

A monument in Lima to General José de San Martín

Independence

At the beginning of the nineteenth century, revolts against Spain led to independence for many South American countries, but royalist Peru remained loyal to the Spanish Crown. Resentment existed though, not only among the Native Americans, but also among *criollos*, who were treated as inferiors by the *peninsulares*. Few *criollos* held high positions, and their farming and trading activities were affected by heavy taxes and restrictions. The turning point was the arrival of General José de San Martín of Argentina. The general had freed his own country and helped Chile gain independence. Now he was anxious to see Peru do the same. Following a successful attack on Lima, San Martín declared Peru's independence on July 28, 1821.

But the royalists fought back, led by Viceroy José de La Serna. Next, General Simón Bolívar intervened. He had successfully liberated Venezuela and Colombia. In 1822, Bolívar sailed to Guayaquil (in what is now Ecuador) and met with San Martín. But the two generals were at odds. Bolívar was a Republican, while San Martín favored a constitutional monarchy for Peru. No one is sure exactly what one said to the other, but after the meeting, San Martín left for Chile and a self-imposed exile in France. Bolívar, with General Antonio José de Sucre of Venezuela, went on to secure Peruvian independence by defeating La Serna, first at Junín on August 6, 1824, and finally at Ayacucho on December 9, 1824.

Guano and Railroads

Following independence the new nation had almost countless presidents—thirty-five between 1825 and 1865. Many of them were military men. A short-lived confederation with Bolivia under Andrés de Santa Cruz collapsed in 1839.

Economically, Peru at first relied largely on the sales of guano, or bird droppings. The first shipment reached Europe in 1841. The industry was owned by British and French companies, but the Peruvian government gained its revenue by imposing heavy taxes. The dirty job of digging guano was done mainly by Native Americans, though some Chinese workers were imported.

In the 1860s, the Peruvian government of Mariano Prado borrowed heavily against the guano boom, which at that time accounted for more than 80 percent of the nation's income. Part of the money was used to fund a railroad connecting Lima on the coast—via a summit in the Galera Tunnel of 15,693 feet (4,783 m)—to La Oroya, a mining center in the highlands. This new railroad would become the world's highest. The early part of construction was directed by a North American named Henry Meiggs, who engineered a remarkable system of tunnels, bridges, and zigzags to take the line up the mountains. Disease killed thousands of workers, and Chinese laborers were again brought in to help.

The *Yavari*

In the nineteenth century, steamships were brought from England and carried in pieces by mules to the shore of Lake Titicaca. There, the ships were reassembled to carry cargo and passengers across the lake between Peru and Bolivia. The oldest was the *Yavari*, which was launched in Puno harbor on Christmas Day 1870. The original steam engine was fired by enormous quantities of dried llama dung, the most plentiful fuel in the area. In 1913, the engine was replaced by a massive Swedish diesel motor. The *Yavari* was retired from service in the 1970s, but the classic ship is being restored by local engineers. The *Yavari* is in remarkable condition for its age.

It will be used for tourism, and the money generated is destined for much-needed support of the poorer lakeside communities.

Nitrates and the War of the Pacific

When the guano industry declined in the late 1870s, the Peruvian government was unable to pay its debts and faced bankruptcy. Any chance to redeem the situation was lost in a war with Chile. Nitrate, in demand as a fertilizer and for making explosives, was discovered in the Atacama Desert. The discovery led to a dispute between Chile and Bolivia over ownership of the land involved. The Bolivians tried unsuccessfully to tax the Chileans. Peru backed Bolivia and tried to negotiate, but when this failed, Chile declared war on both countries in 1879. Peru and Bolivia were defeated, and both lost nitrate-rich territory to Chile under the Treaty of Ancón in 1883. Part of the Atacama territory was returned to Peru in 1929.

Into the Twentieth Century

Toward the end of the nineteenth century, two political parties were founded. The Civilian Party represented landowners and merchants, and the Democratic Party had a popular program of educational and social reform. Society continued to be dominated by a small, wealthy elite, and the economy was largely under foreign control, first by British companies—which by that time owned the railways—and then by North Americans with extensive interests in mining.

Augusto Leguía y Salcedo of the Civilian Party was elected president in 1908. He altered Peru's Constitution so that he could be reelected, and his second term lasted from 1919 to 1930. He began a program of public works, building roads, bridges, and railroads funded by banks in the United States, and he gave rights to explore oil fields to the U.S.-owned International Petroleum Company. Leguía did not protect the Indians' lands as laid down in the Constitution, he was strongly anti-Communist, and he was ruthless in suppressing opposition. He was deposed by the military in 1930.

In 1924, Víctor Haya de la Torre had formed the American Popular Revolutionary Alliance (APRA). APRA represented the interests of the middle and working classes. It wanted an end to the exploitation of Indians, called for land reform, and wanted all major industries to be nationalized and removed from foreign control. In 1945, APRA supported the successful presidential candidate, José Luis Bustamente y Rivero, but the party was still unable to get its social reforms passed in Congress. In 1948, the dictator General Manuel Odria overthrew Bustamente and subsequently outlawed APRA. Haya de la Torre was permitted to run as APRA's presidential candidate in 1962, but he did not win a clear majority. New elections were held in 1963, and Fernando Belaunde Terry of the Popular Action Party became president.

Belaunde's First Government

President Belaunde tried to tackle some of the country's fundamental problems, including land reform. He started community-development and irrigation projects, and wanted to open up the montaña with major road projects and colonization. But his popularity declined when he allowed tax breaks to the U.S.-owned International Petroleum Company. In addition, guerrilla groups in the highlands were causing unrest. In October 1968, President Belaunde was deposed when the military seized power.

Military Government

The 1968 military coup was a turning point in Peru's history. The new government surprised many people with its social and economic reforms. Unlike most military governments, which tend to be conservative and right-wing, this government was more reform oriented and left-wing. General Juan Velasco Alvarado became president, and one of the first acts of his government was to place many large international companies under government control. Another was extensive land reform. The large plantations, or *haciendas*, were broken up and organized into collectively run cooperative farms. The government also introduced measures to help the urban poor, subsidizing food and giving some people legal rights to the land on which they lived.

Not surprisingly, these reforms were challenged by wealthy landowners and businessmen. In addition, a worldwide oil crisis led to serious inflation, while world prices dropped for sugar and copper, two of Peru's principal exports. Growing discontent and opposition led to repressive measures by the government, including silencing the press. In 1975 General Velasco was replaced by General Francisco Morales Bermúdez.

General Juan Velasco Alvarado

Return to Democracy

The military agreed to new democratic elections in 1980, which gave Fernando Belaunde a second term in office. Peru faced immense problems in the 1980s, both in its economy and from terrorist activities. International drug trade also increased, with Peru growing much of the world's supply of coca leaves used to make cocaine.

President Alan García Pérez at a press conference in Lima

A Latin American crisis began in 1982 when Mexico was unable to repay its international debts. A clampdown by banks on loans to other countries led to a shortage of funds and the need for price increases and wage reductions in Peru. El Niño in 1982 also caused widespread destruction. Much of this was beyond Belaunde's control, but a growing threat of rebellion in the highlands was not. For a long time Belaunde ignored the threat. When he finally sent in his security forces, they acted so harshly that he alienated many of his supporters. Hundreds of people were killed, and up to 2,000 more disappeared.

In 1985, for the first time, an APRA government took office, under the popular and energetic Alan García Pérez. At age thirty-five, García was South America's youngest president. He tried to introduce the economic and social reforms that APRA had long advocated. But the measures he took, including tax cuts, devaluation of the currency, and a refusal to repay more than 10 percent of Peru's international debts, led to economic chaos. Meanwhile, the guerrillas were becoming more assertive, with Lima at times their target. By the end of García's term, the country was bankrupt, APRA was discredited, and the guerrillas had become a real threat.

Border Dispute

Peru and Ecuador have argued over part of their border since the 1820s. The dispute resulted in war in 1941, which ended in defeat for Ecuador and the signing of the Rio de Janeiro Protocol. Ecuador, however, never accepted the protocol, which gives Peru land with access to the Amazon Basin but

Guerrilla Groups

The two principal guerrilla groups are the *Sendero Luminoso* (Shining Path), and the Tupac Amaru Revolutionary Movement (MRTA, right). Shining Path was based on the political ideas of José Carlos Mariategui (1895–1930), founder of Peru's Communist Party. The group was created by Abimael Guzmán Reynoso, a university professor from Ayacucho. He gained the support of people in rural and urban communities who wanted a better way of life. By the late 1980s, Shining Path controlled large parts of the highlands, including some of the main coca-growing areas. It collected millions of dollars in "taxes" from the cocaine trade which helped fund the group's activities. MRTA was named after the last Inca, Tupac Amaru. Its aim was to overthrow the government.

The damage caused by the two groups in the 1980s was immense. It included bombings, looting, kidnappings, and assassinations. Countermeasures by the army, the police, and government death squads were equally devastating. In 1989 alone, more than 3,000 people died in Peru's political violence. Whole highland communities were wiped out. Often it was not clear whether the guerrillas or the government security forces were to blame.

Leaders of both guerrilla groups were captured in the early 1990s. Guzmán, of Shining Path, was imprisoned for life. The groups no longer appeared to be a threat. Or so many thought until December 1996, when MRTA attacked the Japanese ambassador's residence in Lima and took almost 500 people hostage. The terrorists' demands included the release of MRTA prisoners. They freed many of the hostages early on, but the situation was only brought to an end in April 1997 when Peruvian troops attacked. All the rebels and two soldiers were killed. Sporadic bombings and death threats have occurred since then, but nothing to compare with the dark days of the 1980s.

gives only navigation rights to Ecuador. Skirmishes between the two countries occurred in the border zone in 1982, 1983, and 1991. Serious fighting broke out in 1995. A cease-fire was agreed to, troops were withdrawn, and prisoners were exchanged, but tensions remained. Determined efforts to find a solution finally succeeded in October 1998, when the two countries signed an agreement ending their long dispute.

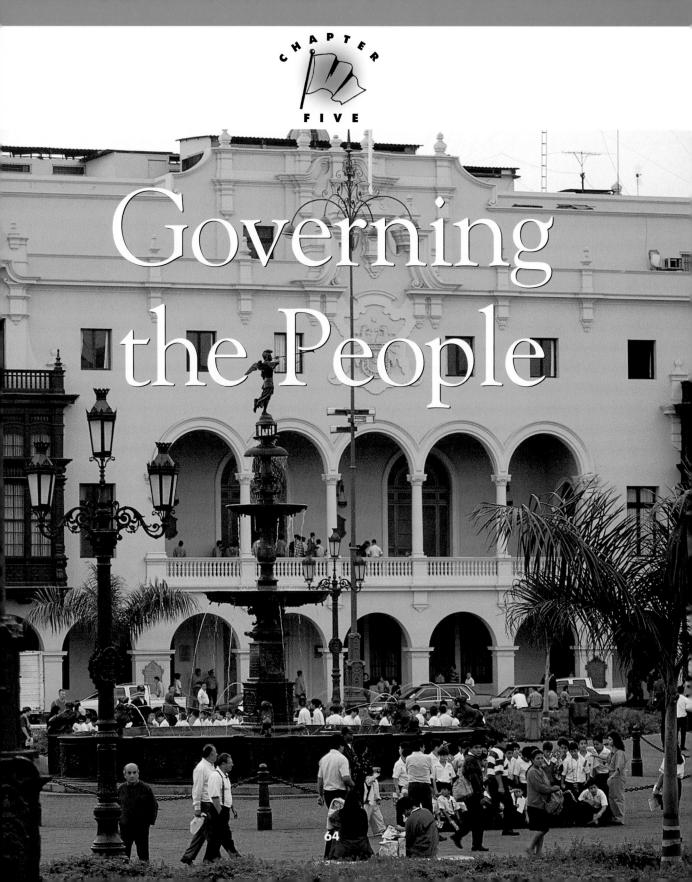

Governing
the People

PERU'S 1990 PRESIDENTIAL ELECTIONS WERE WON BY A UNIversity teacher, Alberto Fujimori. With virtually no political backing, he defeated novelist Mario Vargas Llosa, who represented a right-wing coalition.

Within four years, Fujimori had stabilized the economy. The capture of the guerrilla leaders and the apparent end of terrorist attacks added to his popularity. But he claimed that lack of sup-

Opposite: **Lima's city hall**

President Alberto Fujimori

Lima

Lima: Did You Know This?

Population: 6,022,213 (1995)
Year Founded: 1535, by Francisco Pizarro
Altitude: 512 feet (156 m) above sea level
Average Daily Temperature:

January	74°F (23°C)
July	62°F (17°C)

Average Annual Rainfall: 2 inches (5 cm)

port in Congress hampered him from implementing other reforms, and in 1992 he closed Congress and suspended the Constitution.

This authoritarian approach was a gamble, but it paid off when a coalition supporting Fujimori won most seats in the newly created Democratic Constituent Congress (CCD). He went on to win the 1995 elections with ease, defeating Javier Peréz de Cuellar, the former United Nations secretary-general.

Fujimori has continued to keep a tight rein on affairs in Peru and has been accused of human-rights abuses toward political prisoners and terrorists. There is evidence that terrorist groups are still active, however. He has also continued with a free-market economic strategy.

Dr. Víctor Raúl Haya de la Torre

Víctor Raúl Haya de la Torre was Peru's most enduring politician and founder of its oldest and best-organized political party, the American Popular Revolutionary Alliance (APRA). Born in 1895 to wealthy parents, he became a student leader and was exiled from Peru in 1923 for leading demonstrations. A year later, in Mexico, he formed APRA.

In 1931, Haya de la Torre ran for president but lost in elections that APRA believed were fraudulent. Some of the strongest APRA supporters were sugar workers from the north coast. They organized an uprising in Trujillo that led to reprisals by the army in which more than 1,000 Apristas—supporters of APRA—were killed. Haya de la Torre was jailed, and APRA and the army became adversaries. He was freed in 1933 and lived in hiding in Peru until 1945. He became widely known through his underground activities and writings. Coalition candidate José Luis Bustamente y Rivero, who had the support of APRA, won the presidential election in 1945, giving Haya de la Torre effective control of the government. But in 1948 the government was overthrown and APRA was outlawed.

Haya de la Torre was permitted to run as APRA's candidate for the presidential elections held in 1962, but the results were inconclusive. APRA had the most votes of any candidate, but not a majority of all the votes. Congress was left to decide the outcome. The army, however, did not want Haya de la Torre to be president, and in 1963 new elections were held. Fernando Belaunde Terry emerged the winner. Haya de la Torre died in August 1979.

The Constitution

Peru's present Constitution was proclaimed on December 29, 1993, replacing the 1979 Constitution. According to the Constitution, the president is directly elected by a universal adult vote for a five-year period and is allowed to run for a

National Flag

Peru's flag was adopted in 1825. It has three vertical stripes of red, white, and red. At the center of the white stripe is the national coat of arms. It is divided into three parts. In the top left corner is a vicuña, in the top right is a cinchona tree (the source of quinine, which is used to treat malaria), and across the bottom is a horn of plenty spilling out golden coins. The three images represent Peru's wealth of wildlife, plants, and minerals. Above the coat of arms is a green wreath framed by branches of palm and laurel tied at the bottom with a red-and-white ribbon.

consecutive second term. Executive power is vested in the president. Two vice presidents are also elected. The president governs with the assistance of an appointed Council of Ministers.

Legislative power lies with the Congress, a one-house assembly of 120 members. Each member is elected for a five-year term. All citizens aged eighteen years and older are required to vote.

The Congress building in Lima

Judicial power is vested in the Supreme Court of Justice and other tribunals. The Constitution also provides for a Constitutional Court, made up of seven members elected by Congress for five years, whose function is to ensure that the terms of the Constitution are upheld.

Peru has 24 departments and 1 constitutional province, Callao, near Lima. The 1979 Constitution decreed that regions should replace departments, and 12 regions have been established to date. However the 1993 Constitution limited the authority of the regions, which have yet to assume major responsibilities. At the local level, there are also 155 provincial councils and 1,586 district councils.

NATIONAL GOVERNMENT OF PERU

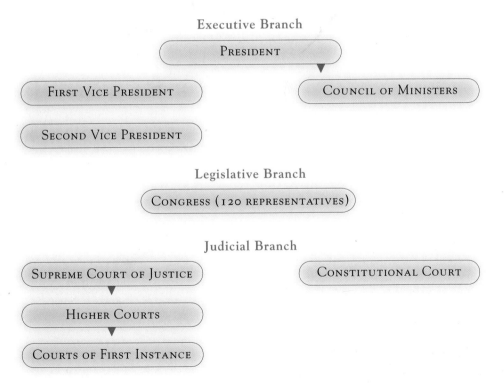

Executive Branch

PRESIDENT

FIRST VICE PRESIDENT

COUNCIL OF MINISTERS

SECOND VICE PRESIDENT

Legislative Branch

CONGRESS (120 REPRESENTATIVES)

Judicial Branch

SUPREME COURT OF JUSTICE

CONSTITUTIONAL COURT

HIGHER COURTS

COURTS OF FIRST INSTANCE

A Struggling Economy

WHEN PRESIDENT ALBERTO FUJIMORI WAS ELECTED in 1990, Peru was in the depths of an economic crisis. The country was virtually bankrupt, with no money to pay its international debts and annual inflation as high as 10,000 percent. Foreign investors turned away because of the guerrilla situation. The huge sums of money made from the illegal drug trade were invested overseas.

Opposite: **Agricultural fields in the Urubamba Highlands**

Since the 1990 election, much has changed, largely due to tough economic measures that included raising food and fuel prices. The diminished threat of guerrilla activity has also helped. In 1994, Peru registered one of the highest annual growth rates—more than 12 percent—of any country in the world. Many businesses once controlled by the government have been privatized, especially in the mining, electricity, and telecommunications industries, and foreigners are again investing in Peru. Agreement has been reached for the repayment of Peru's foreign debt to international banks and organizations. The United States continues to be Peru's main trading partner, handling a large portion of its imports and exports.

Salt drying in pans near Cuzco

A family camps by the roadside while moving from the country to town in search of a better way of life.

A young woman in Lima scans a newspaper's want ads for employment opportunities.

Unfortunately, underemployment and poverty are still widespread. Although the official rate of unemployment in 1996 was just over 8 percent, millions of people have only part-time or odd jobs. More than one-third of the population make up this "informal economy," including many *ambulantes* (street vendors).

The urban poor were hardest hit by the harsh economic measures introduced by President Fujimori, and little has changed for them. In the cities, newly constructed glass-and-concrete apartment complexes, modern shopping malls, and new cars are evidence of renewed confidence, but survival remains a struggle for many people.

Peru is rich in mineral resources. The largest gold mine in South America is not far from Cajamarca, the town where Pizarro demanded a huge amount of gold as a ransom for Incan emperor Atahualpa. Peru is one of the world's major producers of copper, silver, and bismuth, and other minerals include iron, lead, zinc, phosphates, and manganese. Copper and iron deposits are found on the south coast, and the U.S.-owned Southern Peru Copper Corporation produces about two-thirds of Peru's copper at its mines at Cuajone and Toquepala. Copper is Peru's largest export earner.

What Peru Grows, Makes, and Mines

Agriculture (1996)

Sugarcane	6,600,000 metric tons
Potatoes	2,265,000 metric tons
Rice	1,203,000 metric tons

Manufacturing (1995; value added in *nuevos soles* at 1979 prices)

Processed foods	214,600,000
Base metal products	164,600,000
Industrial chemicals	114,200,000

Mining (1995)

Iron ore	3,835,000 metric tons
Zinc	689,000 metric tons
Copper	405,000 metric tons

Oil and Hydroelectricity

Peru was one of the first South American countries to produce oil. It is found in the northwest, on and off the coast, and huge reserves of oil and gas lie in the region of the Camisea in the Amazon. Most of Peru's oil is of a heavy crude variety, but the Camisea deposits consist of the lighter crude oil that the country now has to import.

The many Amazon tributaries flowing from the Andes are a great source of hydroelectric power. Some dams have been built, and hydroelectric power provides about three-quarters of Peru's energy.

An oil exploration camp in the Amazon

The *nuevo sol* (new sol) is Peru's basic monetary unit. One new sol is equal to 100 *centimos*. Peru issues coins of 1, 5, 10, 20, and 50 centimos and 1 sol. Paper notes come in denominations of 10, 20, 50, and 100 sols. In early 2000, 3.52 new soles equaled U.S.$1.

The Torre Tagle Palace featured on the 20–new sol note is perhaps the finest example of colonial architecture in Lima. The palace now houses Peru's Foreign Ministry. There is a strong Moorish influence in the carved wooden balconies and arches, and it has a finely decorated facade and main entrance. It was built in 1735.

Manufacturing

Peru has recently emphasized the development of manufacturing industries. Its factories can produce goods ranging from household machines, clothing, and processed foods to steel, cement, fertilizer, and chemicals. Cars and other vehicles are assembled in Peru. Also, countless self-employed people and families produce goods in small, independent workshops. The government encourages industry in various parts of the country, but most factories have been built around Lima. Unfortunately, this contributes to the city's pollution, which is a serious problem.

A fertilizer plant near Cuzco

Potatoes are a major crop in Peru.

Agriculture

Peru has two levels of farming. Most export crops are grown along the coast—formerly on large plantations and mostly on cooperative farms today. The crops include sugarcane, potatoes, rice, cotton, corn, fruit, vegetables, and olives. The most fertile regions are the river valleys, but large areas of desert are now irrigated and have been reclaimed for growing crops. There are also chicken farms, and many families keep pigs and goats too. Farmers on the coast are well connected by the paved Pan American Highway running north to south, with access to a number of ports.

About one-third of Peru's workers are employed in agriculture, fishing, and forestry. Most farmers live in the highlands, where making a living from the soil is very different from farming on the coast. Much highland farming is at a subsistence level—families grow just enough to feed themselves with a little left over to sell in the markets. Farms in the highlands are small plots, often on the slopes of the mountains. It is not possible to use mechanized vehicles there, so farmers still turn the soil with ox-drawn wooden plows. Seeds are sown by hand, and irrigation is supplied by water draining down terraces cut into hillsides. These slopes were farmed in the same way by the Inca.

Workers harvesting *kiwicha* in the Urubamba Valley

Crops, too, are much the same as those grown by the Inca. They include potatoes, which are native to the Andes, and coffee. Maize is grown on lower valley slopes, while at much higher altitudes quinoa, *kiwicha*, and *kaniwa*, three nutritious grains with high protein levels, have been cultivated for centuries. These cereals are important to a highland family's diet.

Drying coca leaves in Apurimac

For centuries, coca leaves chewed with a mixture of ash and lime have dulled the effects of hunger and fatigue at the higher altitudes. Every highlander carries a pouch of coca leaves. Coca is grown on the eastern slopes of the Andes, and since the 1960s, cultivation has spread across large areas of the mountains.

Coca is also used to make the illegal drug cocaine. The crop is relatively easy to tend, and it brings a better return for peasant farmers than other cash crops such as coffee and cocoa. The price of coca dropped in the 1990s largely because of a crackdown on drug cartels in Colombia. No one is sure how much money the business generates today, but it is probably more than all the nation's legitimate exports combined.

Fishing and Forestry

Fishers clean and sort through the day's catch.

In the 1960s, Peru was the world's largest fishing nation. The main industry was fishmeal exported for animal feed. It was

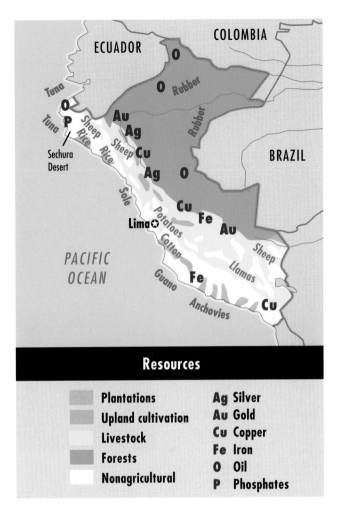

based on the huge schools of anchovy, which thrive in the cold Peru Current in normal years. At the height of the fishing boom in 1970, more than 12 million tons of anchovy were caught. But as a result of overfishing, combined with a serious El Niño in 1971–1972, the fishmeal industry declined. In the early 1980s, El Niño again brought warm waters that drove away the fish, and this time the fishing industry virtually collapsed. The industry picked up again in the 1990s, partly through privatization but also because of larger fish catches.

Peru has huge forests in the Amazon and on the slopes of the Andes. About 100 years ago, the rubber trees were in great demand, but when plantations were established in Asia, the Amazon rubber business collapsed. Synthetic rubber manufacture also hurt sales.

Forests today contain many valuable hardwoods, such as cedar and mahogany, and there is a demand for timber to make plywood and furniture for the domestic market. But the right trees are usually scattered among others, and large tracts of forest are often entirely destroyed. Settlers and businesses also cut or burn trees to make clearings where they can farm

People in the timber industry work together to fell large trees in the jungle.

and raise cattle. Protests against the destruction of forestland have limited the development of a timber industry in Peru.

Tourism

Tourism is the most exciting prospect in the country's economy today. Peru may have more to offer than any other South American nation—stunning ancient ruins; ethnic cultures; glorious scenery incorporating desert, mountains, and jungles; adventure tourism; and a wealth of plant and wildlife species for ecotourists. In the mid-1990s, the number of tourists visiting Peru each year increased to almost 500,000.

Machu Picchu

The favorite destination for tourists in Peru is Machu Picchu (above), set on a stunning site high on a hillside and dominated by Mount Huayna Picchu. It is surrounded by craggy Andean peaks, while far below the Urubamba River winds through a deep forested gorge. The Machu Picchu ruins include temples, palaces, houses, courtyards, prisons, and fountains— everything that makes a city function. Agricultural terraces step spectacularly down the slopes.

To reach Machu Picchu, most tourists take the early morning train from Cuzco. The more athletic walk the 20.5-mile (33-km) Inca trail (left) that lies partway between the two cities. The trek takes three to five days and starts at the relatively low altitude of 9,186 feet (2,800 m). The second day is the hardest, as the trail climbs through Andean passes to a height of 13,780 feet (4,200 m). The effort is well rewarded by spectacular vistas of cloud forest and mountains beyond the summit. Along the route are Inca monuments and terraces, though none is quite so breathtaking as the first sight of Machu Picchu at the final bend of the trail.

People of Peru

PERU HAS A MIXED POPULATION DESCENDED FROM THE original Native Americans, or Indians, and the Spanish settlers and other immigrants who have arrived since the Spanish conquest. These include black Africans, Chinese, Japanese, and various European peoples. Mixed-race *mestizos* are often called *criollos* on the coast and *cholos* in the highlands. Country people—including mestizos, Quechua, and Aymara—are known as *campesinos*. The term *indios* (Indians) is considered insulting.

Spanish dominance—dating from colonial times when the Spaniards were the masters and the Native Americans, the Africans, and others were the servants—began to change as the mestizo population increased. Traditionally, most Indians lived in the Andes and the Amazon Basin, but this too has been changing.

Opposite: **Schoolchildren from Chachapoyas in the highlands**

Population distribution of Peru

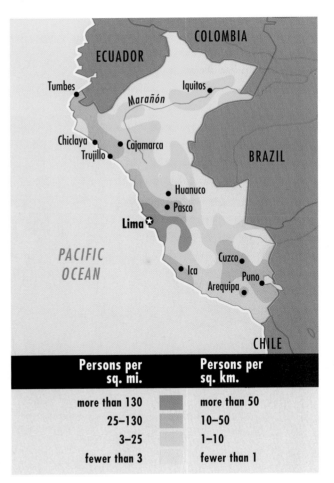

Persons per sq. mi.		Persons per sq. km.
more than 130		more than 50
25–130		10–50
3–25		1–10
fewer than 3		fewer than 1

Who Lives in Peru?

Amerindians	45%
Mestizos	37%
Whites	15%
Blacks, Japanese, Chinese, and others	3%

Since 1960, huge numbers of people have moved to Lima and other coastal towns. It is now often difficult to distinguish an Indian person from a mestizo. As a result, population estimates of highland Indian peoples vary by 3 million to 8 million.

Some 70 percent of Peruvians now live in cities and towns. By far the largest number, about one-third of the nation's population, are settled in greater metropolitan Lima. Other cities, such as Trujillo, Arequipa, and Iquitos, have also grown rapidly. By contrast, the huge eastern montaña and selva regions that cover almost two-thirds of the country are home to only about 5 percent of the population.

Most Peruvians live in cities and towns.

European Immigrants

For more than 400 years, the small, exclusive Spanish white elite exerted power in Peru far outweighing their number. They were wealthy landowners, successful businessmen, high-ranking politicians, and powerful military leaders. With the breakup of the *haciendas* (plantations) and the colonial feudal system that existed well into the twentieth century, the old Spanish families lost much of their wealth and power. However, they remain very much part of Peruvian society. Some have large, generations-old houses, filled with relics of colonial history and family tradition. They employ a staff to run the house, meet at private clubs, and send their children abroad to be educated.

A white Peruvian couple from Lucanas

Other European immigrants arrived from France, Germany, Italy, and Great Britain in the late nineteenth century. Most integrated into Peruvian society, becoming successful farmers and businessmen. Few of these foreign communities retained their national identity or customs. The descendants of Austrian-German families who settled at Pozuzo in the central highlands in 1859 are an exception. In this remote area, some of the inhabitants still speak a form of old German, and some buildings are reminiscent of Austria's Tyrol region.

Mestizos

Most of the middle- and working-class people in Peru are mestizos. Their lifestyle, the type of job they do, and the kind of house they live in depend largely on the education they receive and how much money they earn. The more successful have professional, administrative, and managerial jobs. They work as teachers, lawyers, doctors, civil servants, and politicians—former president Alan García is a mestizo. They run businesses and shops, and they are involved in the media in TV, films, and journalism.

The less-well-off mestizos mostly do manual labor and need more than one job to get by. Men may mix working on construction sites with driving taxis part-time and gardening in their spare time. Women run the family home and also do paid work, perhaps as maids or cleaners. Many families have stalls on city streets and in the markets where they sell everything from religious trinkets to the latest in designer clothing. Children are expected to help and, when they are not at school, earn money by cleaning shoes and cars and doing odd jobs.

In Peru, it is possible to become a mestizo by choice, and many people migrating from rural areas to the cities do just that. Their background may be Native American, but by learning Spanish and dressing in Western-style clothes, they assume the mestizo culture. Arriving in the cities without qualifications or education, they hope for a better life and opportunities. Sadly, most join the ranks of the urban poor.

The Quechua

The Quechua live in every part of the Peruvian highlands except the region around Lake Titicaca, which is home to the Aymara. The most traditional Quechua live in remote villages some distance from a town that they visit only occasionally to do some trading. But many own radios, which provide them with news, entertainment, educational programs in Quechua and Spanish, and—especially—music. Most important, radios put them in touch with the rest of the country in a way they never used to be.

Quechua homes are made of adobe mud brick or stone with roofs of tile or thatch made from tough mountain grasses. Inside are just a few basic items—aluminum pots and pans and maybe a wooden bed with a mattress of split reeds. Otherwise, families sleep on mud platforms and cover themselves with sheepskins and blankets. Cooking is done on an open fire built on a platform inside the hut, or in a clay oven outside.

Quechua men wear knee-length trousers and roughly woven shirts; a wide woven belt; sandals, usually made of rubber from old tires; a large poncho; and a felt hat.

Population of Major Cities (1995 est.)	
Lima	6,022,213
Arequipa	725,838
Chiclayo	686,066
Callao	684,135
Trujillo	627,553

Quechua men dressed in the traditional knee-length trousers, poncho, and felt hat

Quechua women and children dressed in a mix of traditional and contemporary clothes

Quechua women wear a full skirt gathered at the waist over several petticoats; a bodice or short jacket; sandals similar to the men's; a shawl, or *aguayo*, draped over one shoulder, which is used to carry a baby or farm produce; and either a simple felt hat or one with elaborate colored decorations and, perhaps, sequins and tassels. The style of hat changes from one village to the next. Working clothes tend to be in the natural colors of llama or sheep wool, but clothes worn for fiestas are colorful, highly patterned, and heavily embroidered. This style of dress is gradually changing to modern cardigans and sweaters; manufactured shoes, including sneakers; and Western-style trousers and jackets.

Most Quechua are farmers or herders. At the higher mountain elevations, in the cold *punas*, they raise llamas and alpacas and grow potatoes, quinoa, and a few other crops. At lower altitudes, which reach to the subtropical zone, the main crops are maize and coca. Life revolves around the farming year, with seasons for planting and harvesting. Celebrations are usually connected to the farming year, a family event, or a religious festival.

Quechua communities are based on an extended family unit or *ayllu*, a way of life that dates back to the Inca. All members of an ayllu help one another with work such as building homes and plowing, sowing, and gathering the harvest. On these occasions, food and drink are supplied by the grateful host and hostess.

A young Morochuco woman from Pampas de Cangallo

The Morochuco

The Morochuco are unlike any other group of Quechua. Many of them are tall and light-skinned, with light-colored eyes, and many men have beards—most other Quechua men do not have facial hair. They live on the Pampas de Cangallo, not far from the city of Ayacucho. They are excellent horsemen and prefer working with cattle to raising crops. Children are accomplished horseback riders from an early age, and women join the men galloping across the pampa to catch bulls.

Morochuco women racing bareback

Morochuco men wear long, dark-colored ponchos over brightly colored thick woolen tights and sandals. They wear the typical Native American *chullo*—a woolen hat with flaps over the ears—under a felt hat secured with a red scarf. Women ride astride in their full skirts.

Some people believe the Morochuco are descendants of the followers of the Spaniard Diego de Almagro, who was killed by Francisco Pizarro. Riding horses of Arab stock, the Morochuco were seminomadic for centuries, wandering across the land with their animals. They had a reputation for strength and bravery and fought alongside Simón Bolívar in the wars of independence.

The Aymara

The Aymara who live in southern Peru near Lake Titicaca are similar to the Quechua in many ways. However, they belong to a much larger group of Aymara who live in present-day Bolivia. Their ancestors lived on the altiplano before the Inca arrived.

Languages of Peru

Spanish and Quechua are the official languages of Peru. The Inca insisted that all the peoples of their empire speak Quechua, but thirty to forty dialects still exist. This can make it difficult for people from different regions to communicate. Today about 3 million Peruvians speak only Quechua. Many more speak both Quechua and Spanish. Aymara is spoken by people in the Lake Titicaca region, and the forest tribes have their own languages.

The Spanish alphabet has 28 letters. Consonants are mostly similar to those in English, with some exceptions. Spanish does not have k or w, but does include the letters ch as in "chair"; ll, like the "y" in "yacht"; ñ as in "onion"; and rr, well rolled.

Other differences in pronunciation include b, which sounds like "v"; c is like "s" before "e" and "i"; d within a word is pronounced "th" except after "l" and "n" when it is "d"; h is not pronounced; j is like "h" in "happy"; and qu sounds like "k."

Quechua is a complex language, but it is interesting to see a few examples alongside Spanish and English:

English	Spanish	Quechua
How old are you?	¿Cuantos años tienes?	Jaiq'a watayoq kanki?
Where do you live?	¿Donde vives?	Maypin tiyanki?
I am sick.	Estoy enfermo.	Onq'osianin.
Where do you come from, sir?	¿De donde es Usted, Señor?	Maymantataq kanki taytay?
I'm from the United States.	Yo soy de Los Estados Unidos.	Estados Unidosmantan kani.
Since the moment we fell in love	Desde el momento en que nos quisimos	Kuyanakusqanchikmantapacha

The altiplano is a high, cold, and barren place that provides the Aymara with few crops and little pasture for animals. This is the poorest part of Peru, and the Aymara have a hard life. The people who live close to the lake are better off because they benefit from irrigation and can grow more crops, including maize, beans, and vegetables. Some now own two-story brick houses alongside the lake and send their children to school in the nearby town of Puno.

Most unusual are the Aymara who live on floating islands made from the totora reeds that grow around the edge of the lake. They also use the reeds to build their homes, to make matting that they sell, and to make their balsa boats. The islands are so popular with tourists that a post office has been opened from which they can send mail. But encouraging tourists to visit the islands is a sensitive matter. While it provides the islanders with income, it is an intrusion into the lives of this reserved and private community.

The Asian Community

Two principal groups of Asians have settled in Peru—the Chinese and the Japanese. The Chinese came in the nineteenth century to work in the guano industry and on the Central Railway. Thousands died of diseases but some stayed, later setting up their own businesses. Altogether, ethnic Chinese in Peru total about 200,000. It is impossible to walk through a Lima street today without coming upon a *chifa* (Chinese restaurant). There is a Chinese district in the capital, and in towns and cities throughout Peru Chinese families run profitable businesses, shops, and restaurants.

Most of the Japanese arrived in the early twentieth century. Today, they number about 100,000. They have not always been popular, isolating themselves from the rest of the community and remaining loyal to Japan. World War II was a difficult time, when many Japanese were suspected of harboring guns and were deported. However, much has changed with the election of President Fujimori and the appointment of several Japanese Peruvians to responsible government posts.

Afro-Peruvians

Only small numbers of African slaves were brought to Peru, compared with other parts of South America. They arrived first in the sixteenth century, to work as domestic servants in

A Peruvian of African descent

Spanish households. Later, they worked as laborers on the coastal sugar and cotton plantations.

The abolition of slavery in 1854 brought freedom, but the former slaves had neither the education nor the money to improve their lives. They continued to work the land, and today small Afro-Peruvian communities—about 3 percent of Peru's population—live in a Lima suburb and a few miles south along the coast. Their influence on Peruvian culture has been considerable, though, in the fields of music, food, and sport.

Forest Indians

Native American peoples living in the montaña and the selva were much less affected by the Spanish conquest than the highland Indians were. Some missionaries reached these remote areas, but their first real clash with Western civilization came with the Amazon rubber boom. Atrocities were committed against the Indians, and by the end of the rubber boom in 1912, dozens of tribes had disappeared or been largely eliminated

The twentieth century was not kind either. Settlers, farmers, ranchers, and oil companies all encroached on the forest Indians' land. One or two new tribes have been contacted, such as the Nahua in 1986, and others have almost certainly retreated farther into the forest. The Ashaninka were caught up in the guerrilla war when the Shining Path troops invaded their lands. Many were forced to flee, and others starved when hunting in their forest region became impossible.

A secluded Indian family and their house in the forest

Campa Indians fishing with bows and arrows

The Ashaninka, also known as the Campa, live in the *montaña*, as do the Machiguenga, the Piro, the Shipibo-Conibo, and the Amahuaca. Most have contact with mestizo communities in the region, and some have elementary schools and a medical center. The Shipibo are often seen in Iquitos and Pucallpa with their pottery and cloth, decorated with geometric patterns, and jewelry made of beads and glass.

The forest Indians build their houses of split palm wood and leaves. They keep small gardens where they grow crops, especially *yuca*, a white root vegetable similar to the potato. They also hunt, though nowadays more often with a gun than with the traditional bow and arrow. A common form of dress for women is the ankle-length *cushma*, a type of tunic with holes for the head and arms. Cushmas are woven from wild cotton. The Indians paint their bodies with dyes made from plants of the forest such as the red *achiote* and the black *genipa*.

This Yagua Indian is carving a blowgun mouthpiece.

Native Americans of the low-lying Amazon rain forests live close to rivers and rely on canoes to move from one place to another. These tribes include the Nahua, the Matsés, the Yagua, and the Huitoto. Their lifestyle has remained more primitive than that of other forest people, though they too have contact with mestizo traders. The forest provides materials for their homes and their food, as well as medicinal plants to cure illness. They retain their strong belief in the spirit world around them and hold frequent festivals in honor of their gods. At these times, they paint their bodies with lavish designs, fortifying themselves with large amounts of a strong alcoholic drink made from manioc, and dance for many hours to the music of flutes and drums.

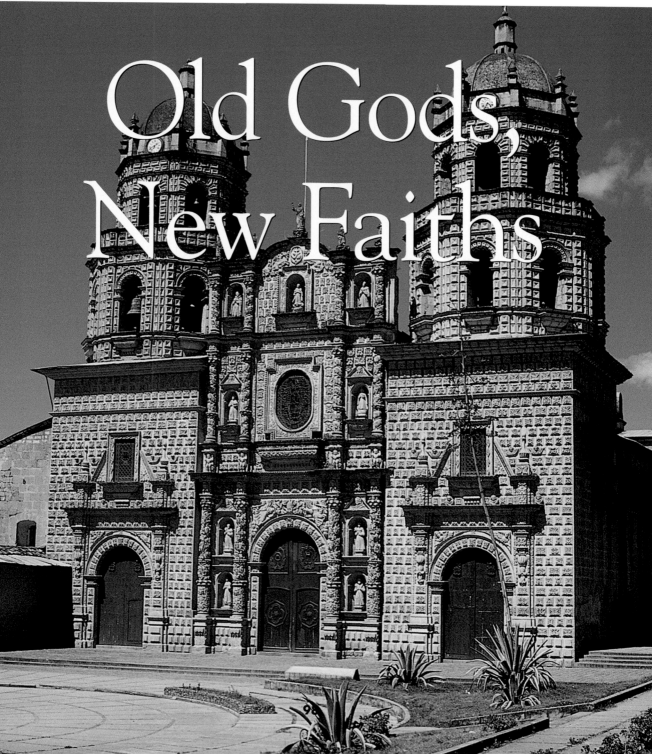

Old Gods, New Faiths

In Peru there are small churches as well as grand cathedrals.

I N PERU, WHERE THERE ARE PEOPLE, THERE IS SURE TO BE A church. Grand cathedrals stand in fine plazas in the cities. Rustic churches of adobe are found in tiny Andean villages, and in the selva even modest settlements have a wooden church.

Christianity was taken to Peru almost five centuries ago. When Francisco Pizarro established his first toehold in the northern desert, he called the spot San Miguel de Piura. The name came from the Spanish for Saint Michael and a name used by the local Native Americans. It was here that the first Christian altar

Religions of Peru*

Roman Catholic 92.5%
Protestant 5.5%
*Does not total 100%

Opposite: **A church in Cajamarca**

was built and the first mass observed. Pizarro and the scores of Spanish priests who followed him over the next hundred years carried the Christian message to many parts of Peru.

The Native Americans the Spanish encountered had their own beliefs. These were seen as pagan by the Spaniards, who tried to eradicate them. What is left today is a mixture. Although the majority of Peruvians are officially Catholic, many still hold strongly to their original beliefs. Often there is a merging of the two, one imposed carefully on the other. Historians and anthropologists call this mixing of religions *syncretism*.

The twentieth century brought more changes. Evangelical churches were established in cities and large towns. This new presence, often from North America, is especially strong in the selva, which is still being opened up.

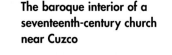

The baroque interior of a seventeenth-century church near Cuzco

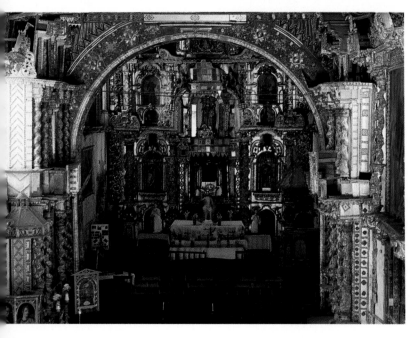

One group that has been active for more than a quarter of a century is the Summer Institute of Linguistics, or Wycliffe Bible Translators. From the institute's well-maintained base near Pucallpa on the Ucayali River, language specialists fly to many parts of the Amazon forest. These dedicated people sometimes spend years with a tribe studying its language. The translators then provide sections of the Bible for the Indians to learn. There is considerable opposition, however, to what they do. In the course of their work, native cultures and beliefs are often destroyed or disappear. The institute also brings many Native American tribes into contact with Western ideas and a cash economy before they are ready to live in a modern society.

Native American Religion

The Native Americans of Peru built many temples and pyramids. Some of these were enormous structures constructed of millions of adobe mud bricks. Others were simpler, perhaps no more than a room with golden figures on the walls. The Native Americans worshiped many gods, including the sun, thunder, lightning, and the earth and its waters. Hills, mountains, and some stones had special significance. The people believed in many kinds of spirits or supernatural beings, some good and some evil.

Offerings of coca leaves and sacrifices of llamas were made at certain times of the year to keep the spirits happy or to keep away bad luck. Much of this original religion was wiped out or transformed by early Spanish priests, but some has survived. In much of the sierra and in parts of the coast, local people maintain many old customs while outwardly practicing Catholicism. In remote parts of the mountains, the original religion is even stronger.

The purest and simplest Native American religion belongs to the tribes of the Amazonian forest. The people in these

The Sun Temple

The most famous of all Inca relics in Cuzco is the *Coricancha* (Golden Enclosure), which once housed the Sun Temple. An 8-inch (20-cm) band of gold was stretched around the entire building at roof level, and the walls were lined with sheets of beaten gold. Inside, there was a large gold image of the sun. Outside, the garden was filled with golden objects, including maize cobs, a life-sized llama, and a fountain. The Spanish conquistadors took all the gold and destroyed the Sun Temple. They built a large baroque-style church, Santo Domingo, on the same spot, and enclosed the Coricancha within a monastery. The entrance today is a church door that leads to a fine, cloistered courtyard where among the Inca remains are the temples of lightning and the moon, and a small part of the Sun Temple.

remote communities believe that supernatural beings abound in the animals and plants of the forest, and in the river, the stars, the heavens, and the earth. For them the influence of Christianity is either newly arrived or, in a few cases of extreme isolation, it is nonexistent.

An Aymara festival of a patron saint

Festivals

In modern Peru, each religion is followed in different ways. Roman Catholics, especially women, attend mass, and everyone celebrates the major Christian festivals such as Christmas and Easter. Older Native Americans of the sierra still make offerings at shrines on certain days, but the younger people are not so involved.

Some festivals are strongly Catholic, but mostly there is a mixing of cultures. In the last weeks of June, in Cuzco, visitors can enjoy both the Catholic Corpus Christi procession, in which statues of saints are paraded around the town, and a pageant of the most important Inca festival of the sun—*Inti Raymi*. One of the greatest festivals in all the sierra is the procession of the Lord of the Earthquakes in Cuzco, which takes place on the Monday of Holy Week. This tradition dates back to 1650, when an earthquake severely damaged many churches. A statue of Jesus known to have miraculous powers was carried through the streets. Soon the earthquake shocks subsided. Since then, the statue, known as *The Lord of the Earthquakes*, has represented Cuzco's patron saint.

Inti Raymi is the most important Inca festival of the sun.

An even greater procession, held in Lima each October, dates back to another earthquake, this time in 1655. The earthquake struck the coastal region, and a wall painting of the Crucifixion survived. The painting—the work of a black African slave—later survived another earthquake and became a legend. Known as *The Lord of the Miracles*, it was paraded around Lima each year. After the original painting was destroyed by fire in 1923, an exact replica was made. The procession, which draws up to 2 million people, combines elements of Catholic tradition with African and Native

The Lord of the Miracles procession is an important religious tradition in Lima.

American religions. It is thought to be South America's largest religious procession.

Andean Mysticism

Darkness arrives quickly in the Andes. As the sun sets, the air cools quickly, and for many months each year the nights are virtually cloudless. The Andean night sky is brilliant with stars, planets, and streaking meteorites, and visitors are captivated by its splendor. Most people just try to guess the names of the constellations. For others, though, the experience is intensely moving, and they wish to participate in the simpler, less frantic Native American life. Their goal is to get closer to the earth and its reputed magical powers.

Mysticism—the discovery of the spiritual heart of something through a communion or quiet contemplation—draws many visitors to Peru today. These travelers seek out the village shamans, or wise men, who are supposed to have the power to cure, to ease problems, or to offer comfort in times of need. Most people pay for these visits. More recently, special tours and conventions have been organized. Some understanding of the Native American religion is provided in group discussions, and then the individuals participate in simple rituals.

Central to many of these ceremonies is a *mesa*, or table, where a variety of small ritual objects are set out, such as seashells, seeds, animal skins, colored sweets, and miniature crosses. They are there for the shaman to "read" and then pass to the spirits. The mesa may be set up in a field, in a home, or even at a church door, according to need.

A Blend of Cultures

THE ARTS IN PERU ARE A BLEND OF TRADITIONAL NATIVE American, European, and other influences. Handicrafts dating to ancient times in Peru, such as weaving and pottery-making, are still created today. Writers and artists may use European styles to portray Peruvian themes. And Peruvian music and dance draw on the sounds and rhythms of the Andes, Spain, and Africa.

Opposite: **Folk dancing at the Raqchi Festival**

A Quechua woman weaving on a back-strap loom

Handicrafts

Peruvians have always been skilled weavers. The materials they use include cotton; llama, alpaca, and sheep wool; reeds from the shores of Lake Titicaca; and palm thatch and reeds from the forests. The weavers and knitters, including men, of the island of Taquile in Lake Titicaca have created a cooperative to safeguard their art.

Quechua people weave on back-strap looms or lay their looms out on the ground outside their homes. Some have spinning wheels, originally introduced by the Spaniards. Women spin yarn while they tend

their animals. Weavings have distinctive colors and designs, often related to a particular village or place. The patterns and symbols represent the natural world, ancient tradition, and myths, as well as modern objects such as trains and planes.

Similar symbols and markings have also been widely used on pottery, ranging from the animals and birds of ancient Nazca to the present-day geometric designs of the Shipibo Indians. Ancient Moche pottery portrayed many human activities, and the Moche are noted for their stirrup-pots shaped like human faces. Vivid colors are also used in both weavings and pottery. These colors traditionally came from vegetable and other natural dyes, but modern synthetic dyes are also used today.

Decorated gourds from Huancayo

Other handicrafts in Peru include wood carvings and jewelry of gold, silver, and semiprecious stones. Decorated clay bulls, symbolic of Spanish times, come from Pucara in the highlands, decorated gourds come from Huancayo, and *retablos* come from Ayacucho. Retablos are small portable wooden altars with carved religious and everyday scenes.

Lima's Gold Museum

One of the world's most extraordinary exhibits of gold is found in the Gold Museum—five underground rooms on the outskirts of Lima. The exhibit includes 14,000 gold artifacts, most of which came from the early coastal civilizations. (Most of the golden treasures of the Inca were melted down by the Spaniards.) Once your eyes have adjusted to the gloom, the enormity of the gold is staggering—both in size and in quantity. In dusty glass cases on every side is a wealth of treasures: masks, items of decoration and jewelry, *tumis* (ceremonial knives), and much more. Most of these objects are up to 1,000 years old. Other artifacts include Moche and Nazca pottery and fine weavings from Paracas.

Writers and Poets

The Inca had no written language. Much of what we know of them comes from the writings of sixteenth-century Spaniards, such as Inca Garcilaso de la Vega and Guaman Poma de Ayala. After Peru gained its independence, in the nineteenth and early twentieth centuries, Peru's most popular writer was Ricardo Palma (1833–1919). His storytelling style was in sharp contrast to the deep thinking of philosopher and writer José Carlos Mariátegui (1895–1930) and Clorinda Matto de Turner (1854–1909). Matto de Turner was a journalist, a novelist, and the first woman editor of a daily newspaper in the Americas. She denounced corruption in the government and the church and advocated equality for Native Americans. Her ideas were considered so controversial that she was forced to leave Peru and spend her last years in Argentina.

Both these writers centered their works on the plight of the Native Americans, a theme first attributed to Gonzalez Prada (1844–1918). The *indigenista* movement that grew from this theme sought to improve the life and dignity of the Indians. For Mariátegui, the answer lay in Marxism—a type of

Mario Vargas Llosa

Peru's leading novelist and an internationally acclaimed writer, Mario Vargas Llosa was born in 1936 in Arequipa. Vargas Llosa wanted to write from an early age, but his father disapproved and sent him to a military college. That experience gave Vargas Llosa the material for his first novel, *The Time of the Hero*. The military authorities did not like the book and burned copies on a public bonfire. Another semi-autobiographical novel is the lighthearted *Aunt Julia and the Scriptwriter*.

Vargas Llosa was a supporter of the Cuban revolution led by Fidel Castro, and in 1969 he wrote *Conversations in the Cathedral*, which portrayed political corruption and was set during the dictatorship of General Manuel Odria. Between 1959 and 1974 Vargas Llosa lived mostly outside Peru. His political views gradually changed, and in 1990 he ran as a presidential candidate for a right-of-center coalition, but lost to Alberto Fujimori.

Vargas Llosa's other works include *The War at the End of the World*, a historical novel based in Brazil, and *The Green House*, which contrasts life in a coastal town with life in the jungle. After his political defeat he wrote *A Fish in the Water*, which tells of his unsuccessful bid for the presidency.

classless society. Other writers such as Ciro Alegría, famous for his work *El mundo es ancho y ajeno (Broad and Alien Is the World)*, looked to the APRA political party founded by Víctor Haya de la Torre. The Indians and their way of life were also central to the work of José María Arguedas (1911–1969), a mestizo who was brought up in a Quechuan environment.

During the second half of the twentieth century, writers moved away from the Native American and rural themes. Cities—especially Lima—and towns provided a new background. Among the most important of these writers are Mario Vargas Llosa, Julio Ramón Ribeyro, and Alfredo Bryce

Echenique, who wrote the popular satire of Lima's upper and middle classes, *Un mundo para Julius* (*A World for Julius*).

Artists

During the early colonial period, artists from Spain and Italy arrived in Peru. Their paintings and sculptures can still be seen in many churches and religious buildings. In the seventeenth and eighteenth centuries, a native Cuzco school of painters emerged. Characteristic of their work are the richly decorated carvings and colorful frescoes in local churches, and paintings that depict religious and local scenes. An unusual painting by Marcos Zapata in Cuzco's cathedral shows the Last Supper with a guinea pig on the central dinner plate. Most of the artists were anonymous, but the best-known Native American painter of the Cuzco school was Diego Quispe Tito (1611–1681).

Mar de Lurin **by Fernando de Szyslo**

Early in the nineteenth century, artists honored the battles and heroes of independence, and later in the century they glorified the great events of Peru's colonial history. In the twentieth century, Peruvian artists, influenced by the social content of the great muralists in Mexico, identified with Peru's Native Americans. The best-known artist of this genre was José Sabogal (1888–1956).

Modern Peruvian art is mainly abstract, notably the work of the painter Fernando de Szyslo and the sculptor

Haircutting Ceremony

Some Peruvian traditions have come down through the generations from Inca times. One ceremony for young children is still followed in parts of the sierra. The "first haircutting" is attended by friends and family from the village. The Inca called the ceremony *rutuchicoy*. Food and plentiful supplies of *chicha*, a maize beer, are provided by the child's parents. The child is dressed in simple clothes, and each adult may cut a lock of hair. Each visitor presents the child with a gift, usually a small sum of money, which is put aside for later years.

Joaquin Roca Rey. Other Peruvian artists now gaining international recognition include Gerardo Chavez, Alberto Quintanilla, José Carlos Ramos, and the sculptor Víctor Delfín.

Music

Andean music from Peru and Bolivia is now famous worldwide. Recordings feature all the highland instruments: harps and violins introduced by the Spaniards; the *charango*, which is a small guitar built into an armadillo shell; Native American flutes and panpipes made from reeds; drums, brass, and wind instruments; and even the conch-shell trumpet. There are also many highland dances. The most popular and universal is the *huayno*, which accompanies a melancholy love song that can be heard everywhere in Peru—on the radio, in public squares, as background market music. It is danced by couples with a vigorous stamping of feet.

Criollo, or coastal, music is very different and has its origins in Spanish and African rhythms. Waltzes and polkas are

Street musicians playing traditional instruments

Peru's national dance, the *marinera*

enjoyed, but the most popular criollo dance is Peru's national *marinera*, a graceful courtship dance. It is accompanied by guitars and the *cajón*, a resonant wooden box on which the player sits and thumps out a rhythm. The late Chabuca Granda was one of the most popular singers and composers of criollo music.

Since the 1950s, communities on the coast have enjoyed a revival of African music, similar to that of the Caribbean. Its strong beat, powerful rhythms, and percussion backing inspire energetic dancing.

Teofilo "Nene" Cubillas Arizaga

Soccer is Peru's number-one sport, and most people agree that Teofilo "Nene" Cubillas is Peru's greatest sportsman. He was born into a humble family in Lima in 1949. From a very early age, Nene was a fan of the Alianza Lima soccer team. He first played for it in 1966, when he was only sixteen years old, alongside another great Peruvian player, Pedro "Perico" Leon. Perico gave him the nickname "Nene" because of his babylike features and his youth. From the start Nene was a high scorer, and in July 1968 he made the Peruvian national team. In 1970, he scored five goals in four games in the World Cup. In 1972 he was voted the best soccer player in South America.

Nene played for European teams for two years before returning to Alianza and teaming up with "Chol" Hugo Sotil. They became known as the "golden pair" for the way they played together. In the early 1980s, Nene was signed up by the Fort Lauderdale Strikers and played in the National American Soccer League. He took part in the 1978 and 1982 World Cups before retiring in 1986. The following year, after all the Alianza Lima players were killed in a plane crash, Cubillas came out of retirement and returned to his old club as player-coach.

In his career, Nene played in 117 international games and scored 45 goals. He received only one yellow card for foul play in his career.

Sports

The people of Peru can participate in virtually any sport. All sorts of mountain sports and water sports are available. Surfing is especially popular, and world championships have been held on Peru's Pacific coast. Peruvians also participate in organized sports, such as soccer, though so far the country has few internationally recognized stars in such fields as tennis, golf, or fencing.

Peruvians are passionate about bullfighting, and the best kind of family holiday is a visit to the bullring. Lima's Plaza de Acho is the oldest bullring in the Americas. It is also a good place to see Peru's *caballos de paso*—the beautiful "stepping horses" whose ancestors arrived on the continent with the Spanish conquistadors.

A bullfight in Lima's Plaza de Acho, the oldest bullring in the Americas

Living and Learning

ABOUT HALF THE PEOPLE OF PERU TODAY ARE CLASSIfied as poor. People living in poverty include most highland Indians, who still follow a traditional lifestyle, and people who live in the shantytowns of Lima and other cities.

In Lima, especially, the authorities have found it impossible to provide housing and essential services for the hundreds of thousands of people who came from rural areas in recent years. They live in ramshackle dwellings made of rush matting, cardboard, or wood, with tin roofing. These shantytowns grew almost overnight on the sandy hills around the city. Some brick *pueblos jovenes* (new towns) have been provided, government programs provide food and medicine, and charities and churches also give support, but it is an uphill struggle. About half of Lima's people live in shantytowns.

In stark contrast to the shanties are Lima's wealthy suburbs. There, families live in large houses protected by guards and dogs. Shops in

Opposite: **Students reading their schoolbooks in class**

Housing in a poor hillside neighborhood of San Cristobal, a suburb of Lima

Miraflores is a wealthy suburb of Lima.

downtown Lima are full of consumer goods and the latest in information technology. Few scenes illustrate the wide gap between the better-off and the poor in Peru as clearly as Lima's city streets.

About one-third of Peru's people do not have nutritious food, clean water, and modern sanitation. There are some wells in the shantytowns, but most people line up at public standpipes to get water.

Modern medical services, such as hospitals and medical clinics, are also in short supply. In the countryside, especially, many people rely on local herb doctors, or *curanderos*, who use herbs and plants to treat illnesses.

A village *curandero* and his herbal remedies

A mother's club in Lima gives lessons on health and disease.

The government has been carrying out extensive vaccination programs, particularly against tuberculosis and diphtheria, but diseases such as yellow fever and malaria still exist in tropical areas. In 1991, an outbreak of cholera—part of a South American epidemic—caused many deaths in Lima's shantytowns.

School students protesting forest destruction

Playing *Ligas*

To play the game of *ligas*, you need a very long piece of knotted elastic. Two children stand opposite each other with the elastic around their ankles, forming a rectangle. A third child jumps in and out of the rectangle, sometimes on just one leg, sometimes on both, and sometimes with legs crossed or with alternate jumps on each side of the rectangle. The jumps follow a pattern, and if you make a mistake, you are "out."

Education

Most schools in Peru are state-run. Education is free, and children aged six to fifteen are supposed to attend school. Not all children do attend school, however, and those who do may drop out early. In the countryside, children are often needed at home to help with farming and to care for animals. Also, some homes in rural areas are a long way from the nearest school, and there is no public transportation there. In addition, classes are usually taught in Spanish, which is difficult for children whose first language is Quechua, Aymara, or one of the languages spoken by the forest Indians.

Towns have many more schools than rural areas do, but even very young children among the urban poor often have to start earning money rather than go to school. About 25 percent of Peru's children do not complete primary, or elementary, school, and only about 50 percent of children go on to secondary school.

Generally, the standards in public schools are not high. Teachers are poorly paid, and schools are under-staffed. Many teachers work in more than one school. Classes are large, and students in some schools attend classes in shifts of morning and afternoon sessions. There are shortages of text-books, pens and pencils, sports equipment, and even desks and tables. Private schools in Lima and other cities offer better opportunities for those who can afford them.

College students in Cuzco

The University of San Marcos in Lima, founded in 1551, is the oldest university in the Americas, and there are universities and colleges in all the major towns. College students are often active in politics, however, and the universities have frequently been closed because of student strikes or government orders.

Communications

Radio and television have made a huge difference to people living in remote parts of Peru. Most households have a radio, and many have access to television or cable TV, even if they do not own one. Today, isolated communities can receive the latest news as it happens, while in the past it took days for news to spread from the coast to the interior of Peru.

Newspapers and magazines are published in Lima and in some other towns, but getting them daily to other parts of Peru has always been difficult, even with airplanes. The leading newspaper, *El Comercio*, which was founded in 1839, has a circulation of only 150,000. Instead of buying newspapers, many people browse through the pages of newspapers displayed on clotheslines at newspaper kiosks. These papers carry domestic and world news in addition to sports, gossip, and sensational stories.

A magazine stand displays newspapers for people who cannot afford not to buy them.

Martín Chambi

A marvelous record of life in Cuzco and the surrounding areas was made by the photographer Martín Chambi between 1920 and 1950. Chambi was born in 1891 of mestizo-Aymara parents in a small village in southern Peru. As a young boy, he worked in a gold mine in the Carabaya Mountains. There, he met the company photographer, and learned the basics of taking pictures from him. A few years later, he moved to Arequipa, where he was apprenticed to a studio photographer. From there, he went to Cuzco.

Chambi's talent and technique were soon recognized. He became a favorite of Cuzco's landowners and upper classes, photographing their weddings and parties. His work included family portraits, theatrical in their setting and composition, and studies of sports teams such as the 1930 Women's Basketball Team dressed in striped blouses and knee-length skirts, and motor vehicles and cycles in Cuzco streets. His landscapes include Machu Picchu and other archaeological sites, and he was often seen climbing Peru's hills and mountain passes, with his heavy camera equipment carried on a donkey.

Most important were Chambi's portrayals of Native American life. His images of Indians in their homes, at work in the fields, and at fiestas, as well as his individual portraits of Indian men and women are at once sad and immensely dignified. They are beautifully lit and exquisite in their detail.

During his life, Chambi's work was known in Peru through postcards, a medium he pioneered. Chambi died in 1973.

Television has a large following, especially the soap operas. They are imported from Mexico, Venezuela, and Brazil, and recently some Peruvian directors have begun to produce their own. Almost as popular are talk shows, comedy shows, cartoons, and programs and films imported from the United States.

The station stop for Machu Picchu

Transportation

Getting from here to there in Peru has never been easy. The Andes make a formidable barrier between the coast and the eastern forests. The Inca built roads, the Spanish introduced horses, and in

Peki-pekis

A variety of watercraft litters the Amazon rivers, from large cargo boats to small canoes propelled by paddle power. There are riverboats with one, two, or three decks, and there are *peki-pekis*. Taking their name from the noise of their motors, peki-pekis are the "river taxis" of the Amazon. They run regular routes along its tributaries, carrying passengers and cargo.

the nineteenth century, work began on the world's highest railway. But not until the first airplane flights in the 1920s did the real possibility of good communication begin. Today, a regular system of flights covers every part of Peru.

Roads have never been an easy way to get from one part of the country to another. The paved Pan American Highway runs parallel to the coast, part of a road network that links Alaska to Cape Horn, at the southern tip of South America. But roads in the mountains are constantly exposed to such problems as landslides and floods. The highest mountain passes are very narrow and rough, and often only surefooted llamas, donkeys, and mules or people on foot or on bicycles can cope with them.

There are no roads at all in the Amazon lowlands. Ambitious plans exist, and perhaps one day a road will link the Pacific coast of Peru with the Atlantic coast of Brazil. For now, though, travel and transport in Amazonia are strictly by boat or by air.

Food

What people eat in Peru largely depends on where they live. In the Amazon region, freshwater fish—from large catfish to razor-toothed piranhas—are very tasty. Fish are boiled or grilled and served with rice or yucca. Bananas are eaten in every form and at every meal—fried, mashed, or grilled—and banana leaves are stuffed with fish or maize and baked. A delicacy is hearts of palm, or *palmito*, eaten as a vegetable. There is plenty of fruit, including all the well-known citrus varieties

as well as papayas, paw-paw, mangoes, custard apples, and *maracuya*, a passion fruit used to flavor ice cream or turned into a delicious drink.

The cold, high Andes demand a very different diet, and soups and stews are the most nourishing and most popular foods. Everything goes into them—meat, including beef, lamb, or *charqui* (dried meat); corn; carrots; beans; many kinds of potato; hot peppers; and spices, especially the very hot *aji*. Because of the high altitude these dishes are cooked for hours and hours. Scurrying around the floors of most Native American homes are small *cuy* (guinea pigs), which are eaten fried or grilled, usually on special occasions. They also appear on restaurant menus. Cuy were a favorite food for centuries before the Spaniards arrived.

Bananas and plantains for sale at a market in Iquitos

The Potato

The potato originated in the Andes, where there are some 150 varieties. They are yellow, white, purple, and red, and they come in all sizes and shapes.

Over the centuries, the mountain Indians have devised a way of preserving them. They spread the potatoes on the ground outside their huts and stamp on them to squeeze out the water. The potatoes are then left out for several days, in the freezing night temperatures and the hot daytime sun. They can be kept for many months and revived by boiling in hot water. In its dehydrated state, the potato is known as *chuño*.

Peruvians have an infinite number of ways of cooking potatoes. They can stand alone as *papa ocopa*—sliced, boiled, covered in peanut sauce, and served with rice, eggs, and olives. *Yacu-chupe* (green soup) has a base of potato to which cheese, garlic, eggs, onions, and herbs are added. *Causa* is a cold casserole of yellow potatoes mixed with hot peppers and onions. Perhaps the most popular potato dish in the highlands and on the coast is *papa a la huancaina*—mashed potatoes topped with a spicy sauce of milk and cheese.

A Peruvian dish of marinated scallops

Fish from the ocean is the basis of many coastal dishes, but chicken, duck, and goat are also eaten. The most famous fish dish is *ceviche*—raw fish marinated in lime or lemon juice, onions, and hot peppers, and served with sweet potatoes, yucca, or maize. *Escabeche de pescado* is fish with onions, hot green peppers, red peppers, prawns, eggs, olives, cheese, and cumin, and shrimp are served as a stew in *chupe de camarones*. Probably the best-known chicken dish is *aji de gallina*—creamed chicken with hot peppers served over boiled potatoes.

Peru's Future

In many ways, Peru is one of the richest countries of Latin America. It has spectacular landscapes—coast, desert, mountain, and rain forest. The Quechua people are one of the most numerous remaining Native American populations. In the Amazon region, Manu National Park is one of the largest parks in the world, with an incredible diversity of animal and plant species. Machu Picchu and Nazca are among the top tourist attractions in Latin America, and the wealth of history and culture of the ancient civilizations and the Inca draw thousands of tourists every year.

Recent years have seen improvement in Peru's economy; a stable, democratically elected government; and a reduction in guerrilla activities. While improving conditions for its large numbers of poor remains a challenge, Peru enters the twenty-first century with better prospects and greater resources than many other countries.

National Holidays in Peru

New Year's Day	January 1
Labor Day	May 1
Independence Day	July 28
National Day	July 29
Battle of Angamos	October 7

The city of Cuzco illuminated at night

Timeline

Peruvian History

Farm people live in valleys of western Peru.	2000 B.C.
People known for weaving and pottery-making live in the mountains and along the coast of Peru.	900–800 B.C.
Chavin civilization reaches its peak.	800–400 B.C.
Nazca culture flourishes on Peru's southern coast.	100 B.C.–A.D. 500
The Moche rule the northern coast of Peru.	100–700
Northern Peru comes under the influence of the Huari.	700–1000
Chimu people create an empire in northern Peru.	1000–1438
Inca people begin an empire in southern Peru.	1200
Inca empire reaches its peak, stretching through present-day Colombia, Ecuador, Peru, Chile, Bolivia, and Argentina.	1438–1533
Francisco Pizarro becomes the first European in Peru.	1527
Pizarro returns to Peru.	1532
Pizarro gains control of Cuzco.	1533
Inca rulers in exile lead raids on Spaniards but are finally crushed when the Spaniards kill Tupac Amaru, the last Inca ruler.	1533–1572
Pizarro founds Lima as the new capital.	1535
University of San Marcos founded in Lima.	1551

World History

2500 B.C.	Egyptians build the Pyramids and Sphinx in Giza.
563 B.C.	Buddha is born in India.
A.D. 313	The Roman emperor Constantine recognizes Christianity.
610	The prophet Muhammad begins preaching a new religion called Islam.
1054	The Eastern (Orthodox) and Western (Roman) Churches break apart.
1066	William the Conqueror defeats the English in the Battle of Hastings.
1095	Pope Urban II proclaims the First Crusade.
1215	King John seals the Magna Carta.
1300s	The Renaissance begins in Italy.
1347	The Black Death sweeps through Europe.
1453	Ottoman Turks capture Constantinople, conquering the Byzantine Empire.
1492	Columbus arrives in North America.
1500s	The Reformation leads to the birth of Protestantism.

Peruvian History

Spaniards crush rebellion led by mestizo Tupac Amaru II.	1781
José de San Martín declares Peru independent of Spain but fighting continues.	1821
Simón Bolívar's army wins independence for Peru.	1824
Peru's first Constitution goes into effect, declaring Peru a democratic republic.	1827
Chile declares war on Peru and Bolivia over the Atacama Desert.	1879
In the Treaty of Ancón, Peru loses part of the Atacama Desert to Chile.	1883
Burial ground with more than 400 mummies is discovered along the southern coast.	1920s
Víctor Haya de la Torre founds the American Popular Revolutionary Alliance (APRA).	1924
Part of the Atacama Desert is returned to Peru.	1929
Military leaders take control of Peru's government and begin reforms; Quechua is made one of Peru's official languages.	1968
First APRA government takes office under President Alan García Pérez.	1985
Alberto Fujimori is elected president.	1990
Fujimori suspends Peru's Constitution and dissolves the legislature.	1992
A new Constitution goes into effect.	1993
In December, members of the Tupac Amaru Revolutionary Movement (MRTA) take almost 500 hostages at the Japanese ambassador's residence in Lima.	1996
Peruvian troops storm the residence in April, rescuing the remaining hostages and killing all the rebels.	1997

World History

1776	The Declaration of Independence is signed.
1789	The French Revolution begins.
1865	The American Civil War ends.
1914	World War I breaks out.
1917	The Bolshevik Revolution brings Communism to Russia.
1929	Worldwide economic depression begins.
1939	World War II begins, following the German invasion of Poland.
1957	The Vietnam War starts.
1989	The Berlin Wall is torn down as Communism crumbles in Eastern Europe.
1996	Bill Clinton reelected U.S. president.

Fast Facts

Official name: Republic of Peru

Capital: Lima

Official languages: Spanish and Quechua

Cuzco

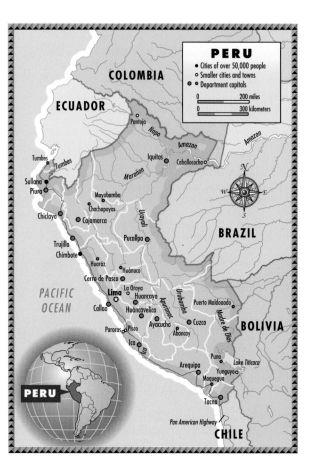

Peruvian flag

A village market

Official religion: Roman Catholic

Year of founding: 1827 (Constitution goes into effect)

Founders: José de San Martín, Simón Bolívar

National anthem: "We Are Free, Let Us Always Be So"

Government: Republic

Chief of state: President

Head of government: President

Area and dimensions: 496,222 square miles (1,285,116 sq km); 1,225 miles (1,971 km), north to south; 854 miles (1,374 km), east to west

Latitude and longitude of geographic center: 10° South, 76° West

Land and water borders: Ecuador to the northwest, Colombia to the northeast, Brazil and Bolivia to the east, Chile to the south, and the Pacific Ocean to the west

Highest elevation: Mount Huascarán, 22,205 feet (6,768 m)

Lowest elevation: Sea level along the Pacific Coast

Average temperature extremes: 47°F (8°C) in January in the mountains; 95°F (35°C) in July in the tropical forests

Average precipitation extremes: More than 100 inches (254 cm) in the tropical forest; less than 1 inch (2.5 cm) in the coastal desert

National population (1998 est.): 25,124,000

Machu Picchu

Population of largest cities (1995 est.):

Lima	6,022,213
Arequipa	725,838
Chiclayo	686,066
Callao	684,135
Trujillo	627,553

Famous landmarks:
- ▶ *Inca Walls of Cuzco*
- ▶ *Lake Titicaca*
- ▶ *Manu National Park*
- ▶ *Machu Picchu*
- ▶ *Nazca Lines* (near Nazca)
- ▶ *The Park of Legends* and *Plaza de Armas* (Lima)
- ▶ *Ruins of Chan Chan* (near Trujillo)

Industry: Peru is one of the world's leading producers of copper, silver, and zinc. Iron ore, lead, and petroleum are other major mining products. Peru's main manufactured goods include fishmeal, petroleum products, refined metals, and sugar. Automobiles and appliances are assembled in Peruvian factories from imported kits. Most of Peru's factories are located in and near Lima.

Currency

Currency: The *nuevo sol* (new sol) is Peru's basic monetary unit. Early 2000 exchange rate: 3.52 new sol = U.S.$1.

System of weights and measures: Metric system

Literacy rate (1993 est.): 87.2%

Common words and phrases: *adiós* (ah-dee-OHS)   good-bye

Schoolchildren from
Chachapoyas

buenos días (BWAHN-ohs DEE-yahs)	good morning
buenas noches (BWAHN-ahs NOH-chess)	good evening/good night
campesino (KAM-peh-see-noh)	Indian/peasant/ country person
¿cuánto? (KWAHN-toh)	how much?
¿cuántos? (KWAHN-tohs)	how many?
¿Dónde está . . .? (DOHN-day ess-TAH)	Where is . . . ?
Gracias. (grah-SEE-ahs)	Thank you.
hacienda (hah-see-EHN-dah)	a large farm or plantation
no (noh)	no
por favor (pohr fah-VOHR)	please
sí (see)	yes
soroche (soh-ROH-chee)	altitude sickness

Famous Peruvians:

Martín Chambi (1891–1973)
Photographer

Teofilo "Nene" Cubillas Arizaga (1949–)
Soccer player

Víctor Haya de la Torre (1895–1979)
Politician

Clorinda Matto de Turner (1854–1909)
Journalist

Ricardo Palma (1833–1919)
Writer

Diego Quispe Tito (1611–1681)
Painter

Joaquin Roca Rey (?)
Sculptor

José Sabogal (1888–1956)
Painter

Fernando de Szyslo (1925–)
Painter

Mario Vargas Llosa (1936–)
Writer

Víctor Haya de la Torre

To Find Out More

Nonfiction

▶ Boehm, David A. *Peru in Pictures*. Minneapolis: Lerner Publications, 1987.

▶ Buell, Janet. *Ice Maiden of the Andes*. Breckenridge, Colo.: Twenty First Century Books, 1997.

▶ Lyle, Gary. *Peru*. Broomall, Pa.: Chelsea House Publications, 1998.

▶ MacDonald, Fiona. *Inca Town*. Danbury, Conn.: Franklin Watts, 1998.

▶ Martell, Hazel. *Civilizations of Peru: Before 1535*. Austin, Tex.: Raintree/Steck Vaughn, 1999.

▶ McMullen, David. *Mystery in Peru: The Lines of Nazca*. Austin, Tex.: Raintree/Steck Vaughn.

▶ Parker, Edward. *Peru*. Austin, Tex.: Raintree/Steck Vaughn, 1997.

Websites

▶ **CIA World Factbook 1999**
http://www.odci.gov/cia/
publications/factbook/pe.html
Facts and statistics on Peru,
including geography, history,
people, government, economy,
and an up-to-date map.

▶ **Cultures of the Andes**
http://www.andes.org/
bookmark.html
Lists many Andean links, including
categories in music, history and
archaeology, languages, and more.

▶ **Martín Chambi**
http://www.garnet.berkeley.edu/
~dolorier/Chambidoc.html
This tribute to photographer Martín
Chambi includes a selection of his
historical photographs. In Spanish.

▶ **Peru Explorer**
http://www.peru-explorer.com/
An online guide to many aspects of
Peru, including tourist information,
outdoor interests and activities, people
and culture, and excellent photos.

▶ **SIL International**
http://www.sil.org/
Official website of the Summer
Institute of Linguistics. Displays
information found in research of
many different language communities.

Embassy

▶ **Embassy of Peru**
1700 Massachusetts Avenue NW
Washington, DC 20036
(202) 833-9860
http://www.embassy.org/embassies/
pe.html

Index

Page numbers in *italics* indicate illustrations.

Meet the Author

"**I**STUDIED HISTORY IN COLLEGE AND SINCE THE 1960S HAVE traveled widely in Peru. I have lived in Lima and Cuzco and have many friends in these cities. My extensive travels in other parts of South America have provided a good perspective on life in Peru, one of the first South American countries I visited.

"From the moment I stepped foot in the Peruvian Andes I was fascinated by the mixing of two cultures. I feel extremely lucky to look back to the village life I experienced at the beginning of my travels because so many changes are happening today. At one time a radio was a rarity, but now they are everywhere and television is quickly following, often via satellite. Even the cellular phone has arrived in many places. Small

towns usually have a local computer expert and can hook up to e-mail.

"Travels with my zoologist husband took me to the Manu River only months after it was first identified as a fabulously rich reserve of wildlife. In one period of a year I saw much of the country by road, camping most of the time.

"At home we keep a house full of clippings from papers and magazines, many of them from South and Central America. We have a small library of books, and in London I can access the latest economic data. We are members of several organizations strongly involved with Latin America and continue to travel there regularly."

Photo Credits